Duke Ellington

D0027241

Washington Wobble

Of all the millions he encountered through his life, the person who had the most profound influence on Duke Ellington was his mother. *Because of the fact that no one else but my sister Ruth had a mother as great and as beautiful as mine, it is difficult to put into understandable words an accurate description of my mother, Daisy,* he wrote near the end of his life.[1] His father also won his admiration: *He was a party man, a great dancer (ballroom, that is), a connoisseur of vintages, and unsurpassed in creating an aura of conviviality.*[2] These special people, James Edward Ellington and Daisy Kennedy, were married on 3 January, 1898. A first child died in infancy, but on 29 April, 1899, Edward Kennedy Ellington was born at his father's parents' house, 2129 Ward Place, NW, Washington, DC, which the young family made their home, too.

Their part of the North West quadrant of Washington, with its social and commercial artery along U Street, was the most prosperous of the African-American neighbourhoods in a city with around 30 per cent of its population black. Many blacks from the South were attracted to the national capital with the emancipation of the slaves at the end of the Civil War: it was within easy reach and there were jobs. 'A large proportion of these people had been drawn to Washington because they felt they could lead a life of ease there,' wrote the black educator Booker T Washington, describing the period after the Civil War. 'Others had secured minor government positions, and still another large class was there in the hope of securing Federal positions.'[3] Others found work as domestic servants or in the city's

Controlled by congressmen largely from states where African-Americans were free, the District of Columbia became a haven for liberated blacks from slave states and the centre of African-American intellectual, cultural and business life. But segregationist Jim Crow laws came in and by the 1920s 'the only integration in Washington was on trolleys and buses, at Griffith Stadium (but not on the baseball field itself, of course), and in libraries.' Zoning regulations separated black and white housing as slums were cleared after Pierre l'Enfant's town plan was revived and monumental buildings went up around the National Mall: towards the end of construction in 1930s, Senator T P Gore commented: 'At least they will make wonderful ruins.'

bars and restaurants. However menial the tasks, they were not as hard as picking cotton. Daisy's father was one of forty policemen among Washington's 96,000 blacks, and she was born there. James Edward Ellington – always known as J E or Uncle Ed – had been brought by his parents from North Carolina as a teenager and worked as a waiter, coachman and eventually butler to a successful white doctor with a house on Rhode Island Avenue, NW. In his spare time, he got casual catering jobs in the great mansions of Washington, including the White House itself. Daisy helped by doing domestic work, too, and in 1918 J E was able to lease a house on a fashionable stretch of K Street and make a living from renting out rooms to women war workers. Two years later he bought a house of his own at 1212 T Street, NW, in a good black neighbourhood, and took a Government job in a US Navy blueprint office.

Meanwhile young Edward was growing up *pampered, and spoiled rotten by all the women in the family, aunts and cousins*[6] in a city where the African-American population had the confidence brought by prosperity, and a successful, though segregated, society. Daisy took him to the 19th Street Baptist Church, and the family also went to J E's church, the John Wesley AME Zion Church, then on 18th Street between L and M streets, because it was nearer to home. There were such familiar hymns as 'Rock of Ages' and 'Onward Christian Soldiers', and arrangements of spirituals. The Howard Theatre brought in important black entertainers such as the blues singer Mamie Smith and the soprano Sissieretta Jones, the 'Black Patti', who sang operatic arias and ballads like her namesake, Adelina Patti. Amateur singers were recruited to the Samuel Coleridge-Taylor Choral Society to perform the cantata 'Hiawatha's Wedding Feast' with the African-British composer himself conducting during anAmerican tour. The Washington-trained James Reese Europe left town for New York, formed the Clef Club for black musicians and led the band which backed the white ballroom stars Vernon and Irene Castle as they revolutionised social dancing with the syncopated foxtrot at the beginning of World War I.

J E was a good enough pianist to play for parties at home, and Daisy played pieces *so pretty they'd make me cry*[8]. Young Edward

'Edward, you are blessed. You don't have anything to worry about. Edward, you are blessed!'

Daisy Ellington[7]

started piano lessons with a local teacher, unforgettably called Mrs Clinkscales, at the age of about seven. But it *all slipped away from me*[9], he said later, because his main interests were games and girls. He got a job selling snacks and beer at the major league baseball park, although the Washington Senators were a joke: First in war, first in peace, and last in the American League. As a 14-year-old he started going to poolrooms, and listened to the conversations of lawyers, doctors, dining-car waiters, gamblers, cheats and crooks. There were *handwriting experts who would enjoy copying some-body's signature on a check, go out and* cash *it, and bring the money back to show the cats in the poolroom what* artists *they were. They didn't need the money. They did it for the kicks.*[10] He also heard the pianists who hung out there. Boys under 16 were not allowed in poolrooms or in burlesque houses, but Ellington had been going to the shows since he was 12. And he remembered: *I had been trying to fuck ever since I was six years old. I wasn't doing very much of it, but I was tryin' and it felt pretty good, whatever it was. I finally got it in when I was around about twelve years old, I guess, out in a field someplace, I don't know where it was, I don't know who it was.*[11]

Baseball, football, track and athletics were what the real he-men were identified with, and so they were naturally the most important to me.[12]

Of the only two public high schools open to black students of the time in Washington, one – Dunbar – emphasised academic subjects. The other, Armstrong Manual Training High School, followed the principles of Booker T. Washington, who advocated teaching industrial, craft, and domestic skills to his fellow African-Americans. Young Ellington went there in 1914 to study design and art. That summer or the summer before, while working as a dishwasher as a holiday job at Asbury Park, New Jersey, he mentioned that he had been listening to Washington pianists, and his boss suggested that he stop in Philadelphia on the way home to hear Harvey Brooks. *He was swinging, and he had a tremendous left hand, and when I got home I had a real yearning to play.*[13] Kept indoors with a cold for a couple of weeks, and remembering some of what Mrs Clinkscales had taught him, Ellington worked out his first composition, which he called 'Soda Fountain Rag', because he had been working as a soda jerk. A second piece, 'What You Gonna Do When the Bed Breaks Down?', he described as *a pretty good 'hug-and-rubbin' crawl*[14] He began to be invited to parties, and *I learned that when you were playing piano there was always a pretty girl standing down at the bass clef end.*[15]

Already he had acquired the nickname Duke, partly from the similarity of Ellington to Wellington, but mainly because he had assumed a precociously courtly attitude and style of dress. His mentor was his father: 'He was beautiful,' said the drummer Sonny Greer, 'he was something else.'[16] Duke himself recalled the

The suave, sophisticated image that Ellington projected in the late 1930s

gallantry of his father's conversations with women, and imitated them: *'Gee, you make that hat look pretty,' he would say . . . Whatever place he was in, he had appropriate lines. 'The millions of beautiful snowflakes are in honour of your beauty,' he declared in Canada.*[17]

The pianists Ellington heard were playing the local variety of ragtime, a brightly rhythmic two-beat style which different players could adapt to their own styles, incorporating dance tunes, classical pieces and their own improvisations. *Those Washington pianists sounded so good to me! And they looked so good! Particularly when they flashed their left hands . . . So I developed a flashy left hand*[18] Some played by ear, others were schooled musicians, and Ellington was taken under the wing of the versatile Oliver 'Doc' Perry, learning from him and later substituting for him when he had two dances to play at the same time. Another pianist, Louis Thomas, employed him and taught him a lesson when he took $90 of Ellington's $100 fee for a job: Ellington decided he could become a manager himself. He turned down an art scholarship to the Pratt Institute in Brooklyn and left high school to concentrate on music, while also using his talent as a commercial artist to help set up a business painting scenery for the Howard Theatre and posters for dance halls. He said that when a customer came in to order a poster for a dance, he asked him whether he would like to hire a band: if a customer wanted a band, Ellington asked whether he needed a poster.

Before I left Wasington, D.C., to come to New York I spent all my time listening to piano players: Doc Perry, Lester Dishman, Louis Brown, Turner Layton, Gertie Wells, Clarence Bowser, Sticky Mack, Blind Johnny, Cliff Jackson, Claude Hopkins, Phil Wurd, Caroline Thornton from Washington, Luckey Roberts from New York, Eubie Blake from Baltimore, Joe Rochester, Harvey Brooks from Philadelphia – and all the others who passed through Washington.[19]

A few months later, in April 1917, the United States entered the First World War. Washington filled up with young people involved in the war effort – Ellington himself, too young to be called up, got a day job as a messenger in the War Department, and later at the State Department – and the demand for dance musicians leaped. Working in other leaders' bands, learning to cope with reading new arrangements and the problems of the business, Ellington started to put bands of his own together and hire rooms to hold dances. A group of friends he could call on when there was work included Otto Hardwick, a saxophone player.

Hardwick recalled that around 1918 Ellington and his friends began to get jobs with white patrons, and often in the suburbs which were usually the territory of 'society' bands. They found themselves playing for the horsy set in parts of Virginia within reach of the capital, horse shows in the summer and hunt balls in the winter. The 'dicty' crowd – the grand people in mansions and embassies – wanted bands for their functions, and they had suddenly discovered jazz, with the release of the first records by the Original Dixieland Jazz (or Jass) Band, a white group from New Orleans which was working at Reisenweber's Restaurant near Columbus Circle in New York. They sound frantic now, perhaps because the band had to rush to get their performances on to 10-inch

Otto Hardwick (1904–1970) pronounced 'Oh-toe', nicknamed 'Toby'. Began playing violin, switched to double bass until his father got tired of carrying it to gigs, and took up saxophone. He soon discovered an extraordinary facility. 'He never tuned up, he never cleaned out his mouthpiece,' said the multi-instrumentalist Garvin Bushell. 'I saw him change a reed one day and I swear, I think worms were in his mouthpiece. He just pushed it back again and he never sounded better'[20]

records, but they launched the Jazz Age. Ellington reacted with an advertisement in a 1919 Washington classified telephone directory offering 'Irresistible Jass' by The Duke's Serenaders, coloured syncopators whose manager was E K Ellington.

By now, Ellington was married, to Edna Thompson, who had been training to teach music. 'It was at Armstrong that Ellington and I fell in love,' she said later. 'He had just learned the difference between boys and girls.[21]' They married on 2 July, 1918, moved to 3rd Street, NW, and then to a house at 2728 Sherman Avenue, NW. A son, Mercer, was born on 11 March, 1919. Ellington bought a car for about $2,000 and claimed to be earning $10,000 a year from his businesses, but Edna remembered them as 'hard days'. She told the same interviewer: 'I taught Ellington and Mercer how to read music. Ellington would be out behind the YMCA football and basketball when he should have been studying.' But as his career expanded, Ellington felt the need of a better musical education and took lessons from Henry Grant, who taught at Dunbar High School. An early biographer of Ellington said Grant recalled that 'harmonising a simple melody was always an experiment in color with Duke; it was always important to him to create a sound that "rang," as he put it, either because it was mellifluous, exquisitely concordant, or because it was bizarre, challengingly discordant.' Hardwick and their friend, the trumpeter Arthur Whetsel, also studied with Grant.

The boom in music in Washington continued. The cornet-player Rex Stewart, then a teenager living in Georgetown before it was a fashionable address, recalled the high numbers of dance halls open to black musicians in 1921: 'Starting with the then spanking new Lincoln Colonnades, there was Murray's Casino, True Reformers Hall, Eye Street Hall, Stack O'Lee's in Foggy Bottom, Odd Fellows Hall in Georgetown, the Woodman's Hall in Anacostia, Eagle's Hall in the Northeast section, the Masonic Hall in midtown, and Convention Hall, plus ten or so smaller halls. There was a dance somewhere every night.'²² Musicians from out of town arrived to work there, among them a Puerto Rican valve-trombone player, Juan Tizol, who had been hired to improve the orchestra at the Howard Theatre. Others were the banjo and guitar player Elmer Snowden, from Baltimore, and the drummer Sonny Greer, from Long Branch, New Jersey.

No recordings were made of the kind of music Ellington and his

Sonny Greer (1895–1982) was in Ellington's bands from 1924 until 1951, a vital part of the act as showman and comedy vocalist. 'Sonny would sit up behind the band, elevated high at his drums, an enormous array of blocks, bells, chimes, cymbals, snares and so on surrounding him, looking like the king of the band'²³

colleagues were playing and it is hard to guess what it was like. In different parts of America a diversity of styles was growing up, and the New Orleans music made famous by King Oliver's Creole Jazz Band in Chicago, with Louis Armstrong playing second cornet, was only one of them, even though it was to dominate the history of what eventually became jazz. Garvin Bushell, a reed player based in New York, described what he heard in 1921 in Baltimore, the nearest major city to Washington: 'They were very fly, smart, creative improvisers. But they didn't play the blues the way musicians from the South did. Their jazz was based on ragtime piano practices, and ragtime piano influenced the way they played their horns.'[24] Ragtime was also the ancestor of the style used by the heroes of African-American music-making on the east coast of the United States, the masters of 'stride' piano. Dick Wellstood, a formidable pianist of the later 20th century, described stride as 'a sort of ragtime, looser than Joplin's "classic rag", but sharing with it the march-like structures and oom-pah bass.' In the work of James P Johnson, Fats Waller, Willie 'The Lion' Smith, Eubie Blake, Luckey Roberts, and Donald Lambert, Wellstood wrote, 'the feeling of stride is a kind of soft-shoe 12/8 rather than the 8/8 of ragtime, and, although the left hand plays oom-pahs, the total feeling is frequently an accented four-beat rather than the two-beat you might expect.'[25]

Ellington could have heard many stride masters on their visits to Washington, and he had particular memories of seeing James P Johnson, the great New York pianist, at Convention Hall in November 1921. Ellington's fans dared him to challenge the master by playing Johnson's 'Carolina Shout', regarded as a test-piece for aspiring players, which he had learned from a piano roll. He claimed to have impressed James P so much that they went off together on a tour of the South-West district until ten o'clock the next morning.

Rent Party Blues

When Duke Ellington left his native Washington in 1923 to live and work in New York, he found himself among the pioneers of an African-American cultural explosion which became known as the Harlem Renaissance. Politicians, teachers, churchmen, artists and entertainers were founding a community in the north-west part of Manhattan, where there evolved a capital city of black America with room for the rich, the poor and the people in between. Although migrants were drawn there from across the nation, Harlem was specially attractive if you came from Washington, an easy train ride away, because Washington social life was dominated by light-skinned ' high yellow' families, some pale enough to 'pass for white', who shunned and despised darker African-Americans. 'The behaviour of high yellow society was a replica of high white, except that whereas the white woman invested in tightly curled permanents and, at least if young, cultivated a deep sun tan, the colored woman used bleach lotions and Mrs Walker's "Anti-Kink" or the equivalent to straighten hair.[26] It took years for Harlem to become predominantly black. The playwright Arthur Miller, who spent his childhood in his family's apartment on 110th Street, wrote: 'In the mid-twenties, whites were not necessarily vacating houses into which black and Puerto Rican families moved. It was by no means taken for granted that all of Harlem was to be a black ghetto – in fact it was inconceivable when some of the best restaurants in the city were doing great business on Seventh and Lenox and along 125th Street too. The Cotton Club, after all, was deep in black Harlem but largely patronised by whites.'[27]

About 1904 better-off black New York families began to move to Harlem, then a newly-built neighbourhood of tree-lined streets on the outskirts of the city. An influx of African-Americans from the southern states increased in volume when the First World War cut off the supply of European immigrants, opening industrial jobs to blacks. By 1923 New York had overtaken Washington as the city with the biggest black population. Alongside intellectuals such as W E B DuBois, head of the National Association for the Advancement of Colored People, and poets such as Langston Hughes and Countee Cullen, entertainers flourished and overflowed onto Broadway after the musical 'Shuffle Along', with an all-black cast and songs by the black musicians Eubie Blake and Noble Sissle, scored a smash hit in 1921. Two years later Ellington's idol, James P Johnson, followed it with 'Runnin' Wild' which ran for 213 performances and started an international craze with his song 'The Charleston'.

To the general public jazz was primarily a novelty music at the time, its commercially successful practitioners thriving from the surprises or comedy that appealed to vaudeville audiences, and the job that brought Ellington to New York was with a notorious exponent of musical gimmickry. He was Wilbur Sweatman, and his speciality was playing three clarinets simultaneously. At the Lafayette Theatre, a 2,000-seater at 132nd Street and 7th Avenue which would later become a cinema and then a church, he opened on 5 March 1923 with a band, wearing make-up to lighten their faces, which included Ellington and his friends from Washington, Toby Hardwick and Sonny Greer. *I began to realise that all cities had different personalities, which were modified by the people you met in them. I also learned a lot about show business from Sweatman. He was a good musician, and he was in show business because that was where the money was then.*[28] At the end of a week's engagement they had to choose between going on tour with Sweatman and staying on in New York without work. They stayed, lodging with relations and raising cash by playing pool.

Lenox Avenue – now Malcolm X Boulevard – near 140th Street in the 1930s

The three friends were protected and encouraged by one of the masters of Harlem's music, the pianist Willie 'The Lion' Smith, who said he earned his nickname from a French colonel who admired his ferocity as an artilleryman in World War I. Greer claimed to know Smith, who led the band at the Capitol Palace, an underground night-club on Lenox Avenue, and introduced Ellington. *The Lion extends his hand and says, 'Glad to meet you, kid,' –and, looking over his shoulder–'Sit in there for me for a couple of numbers. D-flat. As one of those Western piano plonkers just fell in, I want him to take the stool so I can crush him later,' he adds. This was the great thing about the Lion: a gladiator at heart.*[30] Smith said of Ellington: 'He was always a good-looking, well-mannered fellow, one of those guys you see him, you like him right away; warm, good-natured. I took a liking to him, and he took a liking to me. I introduced him, and

Harlem, to our minds, did indeed have the world's most glamorous atmosphere. We had to go there.[29]

the girls took a liking to him, too.'[31] Ellington, Hardwick and Greer joined Smith's 'wandering gang' of musicians touring Harlem in search of opportunities to play, often in competition with other players in what were called cutting contests. 'There was usually lots of action in Harry Pyle's speakeasy up on Fifth Avenue,' the Lion wrote. 'If there wasn't, we'd keep making the rounds until we found some life – sometimes it would be in some cat's apartment. When we found a lively spot we'd get a fast session under way that would sometimes last until noon. This was a frequent occurrence during the 1920s and 1930s when we met in cabarets, speakeasies, or at the house-rent parties.'[32]

The house-rent party was the cornerstone of social life in Harlem, where people had trouble raising the rent, even before the Depression which followed the 1929 stock market crash. By the end of the 1920s the Big Three pianists were The Lion, James P Johnson, and young Fats Waller, and they would often play at three parties on a Saturday night, alternating with each other, or with lesser players, sending deputies to their regular jobs or joining the party circuit when their club work ended in the early hours. 'Some of the parties spread to the halls and all over the building,' The Lion remembered. 'All the furniture was stashed in another apartment except the chairs and beds. When there wasn't a crap game, or poker, going on in the back bedroom, they'd use it for a place to rest up, or sleep off, or make love.'[33]

On his first visit to New York Ellington began to be accepted and find work at rent parties. But except for Saturday nights there were few chances to earn money, and when Duke found fifteen dollars in the street, the Washington friends bought themselves a meal and train tickets home. When Ellington got to his parents' house, on a Sunday morning, his mother grilled mackerel and his father opened the corn whiskey he made in his own still. In June, though, Hardwick and Greer went back to New York, with Arthur Whetsel and the banjo-player Elmer Snowden as leader, to take a job with Fats Waller as pianist. Waller was nowhere to be found, so they sent for Ellington, and he caught the train, first class. The job vanished, and the group faced weeks of searching for work until Snowden met the dancer Ada Smith, known as Bricktop, later a famous hostess to the rich at her nightclubs in Paris, Mexico City and Rome. Bricktop got the band a job, without salary but with the promise of big tips, at the Exclusive Club, at 7th Avenue and 134th Street. The boss was Barron Wilkins, who operated as a politician and backer of black boxers and baseball teams, as well as running a club for the upper crust of Harlem, most of it white. 'One easily forgets that all Harlem is not like it!' wrote one journalist. 'Harlem, the Harlem of the poor, overcrowded, underfed, with children crippled with rickets and scurvy . . .'[34] The tips were as big as promised, reaching $100 per man per week. Ellington sent for Edna and they rented a room, leaving Mercer with Ellington's parents. Edna found work as a showgirl. The Snowden band moved on to the Hollywood Club with a six-month contract, starting in September 1923 – the following May, Barron Wilkins refused to pay his bootlegger and was stabbed to death outside his club.

The band, renamed the Washingtonians, was to stay for the next four years at its new residency, though with interruptions: the proprietor occasionally told the musicians to take their instruments home, and when they turned up for work the next evening they would find that a fire had wrecked the premises, which would reopen after the insurance policy paid out. At one point the name was changed to Club Kentucky, always referred to as the Kentucky Club. It was a tiny basement with a ceiling so low that the band could not stand up, and Willie 'The Lion' Smith compared the dressing rooms to the Black Hole of Calcutta. But the location was all: on 49th Street between 7th Avenue and Broadway, where white audiences spilled out of the Times Square theatres and movie houses to continue their nights on the town.

Snowden moved on to another job in February 1924, leaving Ellington as leader: he soon brought in Fred Guy to play the banjo. Switching later to guitar, he would stay with the band for a quarter of a century.

But already the nature of the band had been changed by newcomers in the brass section. Two extraordinary musicians brought with them a savage intensity which became an essential part of the Ellington sound. The trumpeter Bubber Miley and the trombonist Charlie Irvis both used combinations of mutes to produce instrumental imitations of the human voice in the great tradition of African-American music. To white audiences in the 1920s the sounds seemed to come from a primitive world: they called it 'jungle music' A review of the Washingtonians – written by Abel Green, who later edited the show business paper 'Variety' – said: 'This colored band is plenty torrid and includes a trumpet player who never need doff his chapeau to any cornetist in the business. He exacts the eeriest sort of modulations and "singing" notes heard.'[35] Miley was in Chicago, touring with the blues singer Mamie Smith, when he heard the cornet-playing of Joe 'King' Oliver, mentor of Louis Armstrong and a master of 'freak' effects, such as imitating a crying baby. Miley began to experiment with mutes and found out how to make the trumpet growl.

Bubber Miley (1903–32) moved to New York from South Carolina as a child. Otto Hardwick described him as 'a happy-go-lucky, moon-faced, slim, brown boy with laughing eyes and a mouthful of gold teeth,'[36] and said the Washingtonians made him join them by getting him drunk. After leaving Ellington Miley gigged around New York, toured in France and led his own band before dying of tuberculosis.

Miley replaced the sweet-toned Arthur Whetsel, who had decided to return to Washington. Ellington said later: *Our band changed its character when Bubber came in. He used to growl all night long, playing gutbucket on his horn. That was when we decided to forget all about sweet music.*[37] The word 'gutbucket', from the buckets used to collect drips from barrels of liquor, came to mean 'a low-down, nitty-gritty blues style of jazz originally played in gin mills, barrelhouses, whorehouses, and honky-tonks.'[38] Soon Miley was joined by Irvis, his friend and musical partner, on trombone. Ellington explained: *There was a kind of mute they built at that time to go into the trombone and make it sound like a saxophone, but he dropped his one night and the darn thing broke into a million parts. So he picked up the biggest part that was left and started using it. This was his device and it was greater than the original thing. He got a great, big, fat sound at the bottom of the trombone – melodic, masculine, full of tremendous authority.*[39]

Irvis's few recordings with Ellington give little idea of how impressive a player he evidently was – the Ellington expert Eddie Lambert points to the sides he made with Fats Waller in a band called Morris's Hot Babies as showing him in a clearer light –

John Chilton, eminent jazz historian and a trumpeter noted for his work with mutes, explained that the growl effect comes from fitting a small straight mute – a cornet mute for trumpet and a trumpet mute for trombone – covering the instrument's bell with a rubber plunger, the kind used by plumbers, and moving it in and out to affect the tone: 'With the small mute they could go from a whisper by pushing the plunger as tight as it would go against the bell.'[40]

and he did not stay long with the band. His replacement was his friend Joe Nanton, who learned the art of the plunger, won himself the nickname 'Tricky Sam', and provided the Ellington orchestra with its most original and extraordinary solo voice for the next 22 years.

The Washingtonians began to make records in November 1924, and Miley immediately established himself as the dominant player with a solo on 'Rainy Nights' which shines out from an undistinguished band. Two years later Ellington's name was on the record labels and the first sign of an Ellington style emerged

'Tricky Sam' Nanton (1904–1946) was born of West Indian parents in the San Juan Hill ghetto on the West Side of Manhattan. He was, wrote Rex Stewart, 'a gingerbread-colored man, kind of on the squatty side' with a high-pitched voice, 'a fun-lover from 'way back, a practical joker, a convivial drinker.' While other musicians played cards, Nanton read books, and talked knowledgeably on 'such erudite and diverse subjects as astronomy, how to make home brew, and how to use a slide rule. He could recite poetry by ancient poets that most of us never knew existed, and he knew Shakespeare.' From his trombone he got sounds ranging 'from the wail of a new-born baby to the raucous hoot of an owl, from the bloodcurdling scream of an enraged tiger to the eerie cooing of a mourning dove.'[41]

with 'East St Louis Toodle-oo', written by Ellington and Miley and destined to be the Ellington signature tune until 1941. Half of the title comes from a dance called the todalo – Eubie Blake wrote 'Baltimore Todalo'. Ellington pronounced the name 'toadle-oh' and blamed a printer's error for the change. As for the other half, Ellington had never been to East St. Louis, but thought it sounded like the right place. The composition grows out of a mysterious introduction played by a tuba and a low-pitched saxophone, over which Miley uses his plunger to state the bluesy melody: Nanton, without a mute, brings in a jaunty second theme and, after a clarinet solo and passages for the brass and for three high-pitched reeds, Miley and the first theme return.

The following April, the band recorded another Ellington-Miley collaboration, 'Black and Tan Fantasy'. Miley and Nanton together state a dark-hued blues, and continue it with solos after a contrasting theme played by Toby Hardwick. in the then-fashionable 'swooning saxophone' style. Miley returns with a solo, and a dramatic coda quotes the 'Funeral March' from Chopin's B-flat minor piano sonata. The band then left New York on a summer tour of New England resorts, taking with them Edna and Mercer, now eight years old. They returned to the studios in October and recorded the third of this early group of enduring classics, 'Creole Love Call'. Once again Ellington and Miley are named as composers, this time with the addition of clarinetist Rudy Jackson, recently recruited from King Oliver's band – the 12-bar theme is based on Oliver's 'Camp Meeting Blues'. The record opens with three clarinets, and the surprising sound of a woman's voice, singing without words, and using a throaty tone which matches the growl of Miley's trumpet when it takes up the next chorus. The singer was Adelaide Hall, who had become a star in the European tour of 'Chocolate Kiddies', a revue to which Ellington had contributed several songs. She said that when both she and the Ellington band were in another show, 'Dance Mania', at the Lafayette Theatre on 132nd Street and Seventh Avenue, she heard 'Creole Love Call' while standing in the wings, and hummed a counter-melody. Ellington heard her, and took her later to record it. Ellington saw it differently: *We had to do something to employ Adelaide Hall*, he told an interviewer, and added: *I always say we are primitive artists, we only employ the materials at hand . . . The band is an accumulation of personalities, tonal devices.*[42]

The man who got Ellington

Irving Mills (1894–1985) was born in New York of Russian-Jewish parents. Starting as a song-plugger, he formed a publishing firm, with his brother Jack, which became Mills Music Inc. On its books were song-writers including Dorothy Fields, Jimmy McHugh, Harold Arlen and Hoagy Carmichael. *He'd take a good lyricist, tell him, 'Now, this song needs something right here,' and the cat would go over it, and it would come out perfect.*[43] Mills is credited with lyrics to some Ellington songs, including 'It Don't Mean a Thing if It Ain't Got That Swing,' 'Mood Indigo', and 'Sophisticated Lady.'

into the studios, recording for various labels with various combinations under various names, was Irving Mills. He heard the band and began to manage it, as well as publishing Ellington's songs. He advertised Ellington and fed stories to the Press to build up his prestige. And in November 1927 another Mills associate, the songwriter Jimmy McHugh, was at work on a new revue to go into the Cotton Club on Lenox Avenue at 142nd Street. It is a matter of jazz legend that King Oliver turned down the job, believing that the pay was not good enough, and missed a chance that might have saved his career. Another legend, repeated by Ellington over the years, was that his band was late for the audition at the club, but so was the boss, who gave the job to the only band he had heard. Next day Ellington had to go with 'Dance Mania' to Philadelphia, but the Cotton Club's gangster owners warned the Philadelphia promoter: 'Be big or you'll be dead.' He was big enough to release Ellington from the tour, and the band was in Harlem in time for the club's new show to open on 4 December, 1927.

Black Beauty

The Cotton Club advertised itself as 'the aristocrat of Harlem': it catered to the crowd who were packing the Broadway theatres to see the smash-hit black revues, and wanted to get a closer look at African-American life. Elaborate floorshows brought the romance of the South and the jungle to Manhattan for what the songwriter Harold Arlen called the Mink Set from Park Avenue. The entertainers and the staff were black, but the patrons were almost exclusively white. One of the few African-Americans to be part of the audience was Ellington's teenage son, Mercer, sipping lemonade with his grandparents, who had been granted a booth by the management. He remembered: 'The band was all the way at the back in the Cotton Club, in a shell, with a dance floor in front. The dancers came and went through an entrance on either side of this shell out onto this raised dance floor. The stage was set up to represent the Land of Cotton, with a plantation cabin, rows of cotton bushes, and trees that shot up when the show started. On three sides of the floor were swinging garden gates, with primitive archways and vines over them, through which the public came up to the floor to dance.'[44]

Pride of the Cotton Club was the chorus line of light-skinned 'high yaller' girls. Abel Green of 'Variety' reviewed Ellington's first night: 'The big attraction,

The singer Lena Horne, who appeared there in the 30s, said the Cotton Club 'shows had a primitive naked quality that was supposed to make a civilised audience lose its inhibitions. The music had an intensive, pervasive rhythm – sometimes loud and brassy, often weird and wild.'[45]

of course, are the girls, 10 of 'em, the majority of whom in white company could pass for Caucasians. Possessed of the native jazz heritage, their hotsy-totsy performance if working sans wraps could never be parred by a white girl.'[46] Other acts in the hour-plus shows could be equally disturbing. Earl 'Snake Hips' Tucker

Ellington's band in 'Black and Tan' with a Cotton Club style chorus

gyrated his pelvis, rolled his abdomen and trembled from head to foot with 'a menacing air, like a sleeping volcano, which seemed to give audiences the feeling that he was a cobra and they were mice.'[47] Ellington, who accompanied him with 'East St Louis Toodle-oo', thought Snake Hips came from somewhere in tidewater Maryland, *one of those primitive lost colonies where they practise pagan rituals and their dancing style evolved from religious seizures.*[48]

For the patrons who climbed the stairs from Lenox Avenue to this exotic playground there was an extra thrill on the rare occasions when its chief proprietor appeared, having arrived in his chauffeur-driven bullet-proof Duesenberg. He was the fearsome Owney Madden, one of the era's most ruthless criminals, and the Cotton Club was a huge speakeasy where 600 or 700 patrons at a time could sit at floor-side tables or in booths around the edge of the room and guzzle his bootleg booze.

The lavish floor shows, two different ones each night, began around midnight and 2 am. Between them the band played for dancing. The club had a permanent landline for broadcasting, and Ellington's men were heard across America, sometimes late at night on the East Coast, sometimes early in the evening, when families were sitting down to a meal. Listeners noticed that Ellington chose 'sweeter' music for the suppertime audience. But the weird sounds of the 'jungle music' centred on Miley and Nanton were vital to the shows, and new recruits to the band allowed Ellington to increase his range of strange effects and tone colours. The Ellington band had expanded to ten pieces. Arthur Whetsel

Owney Madden, born in Liverpool in 1892, came to New York when he was eleven. Paroled from Sing Sing in 1923 after committing several violent murders he opened breweries in Hell's Kitchen on the West Side of Manhattan and the Cotton Club (above) in Harlem. 'His hair was black and sleek. His eyes were blue, a very bright and piercing blue. Sometimes they were friendly enough, and in repose they were even sad, but usually they were hard, and shining, and they saw everything.'[49] In the early 1930s Madden retired to a tourist resort notorious for illegal gambling, Hot Springs, Arkansas. He died there, peacefully, in 1964 at the age of 72.

re-joined, his sweet tone contrasting with Miley's growl, and the stately Wellman Braud from New Orleans became the first of Ellington's great bass players, 'pulling the single strings up on one beat and slapping them against the board on the next,' Mercer remembered. 'That was what made him swing.'[50] After Toby Hardwick left, a new reed section was formed by three men, all of them destined to be major soloists: Johnny Hodges, Barney Bigard and Harry Carney.

Johnny Hodges (1907–1970) from Cambridge, across the river from Boston, was given lessons by the great New Orleans saxophonist Sydney Bechet. Hodges's rich tone and fluency on alto became one of the most distinctive sounds of the Ellington band on romantic ballads and blues numbers.

Barney Bigard (1906–1980) was born in New Orleans and worked with King Oliver in Chicago before joining Ellington, playing tenor saxophone in the reed section and taking clarinet solos in a dramatic Creole style.

Harry Carney (1910–1974) was Hodges's neighbour in Boston and left school to join Ellington. At first playing alto, he developed into the first jazz soloist to master the baritone saxophone and later the bass clarinet.

During the years when the band was resident at the Cotton Club, Ellington would record his own 'Jungle Blues' and 'Jungle Nights in Harlem', as well as savage titles such as Fields and McHugh's 'Hottentot' and 'Diga Diga Doo'. But his masterpiece in the style, which he was still playing more than 40 years later, was 'The Mooche'. Its earliest version, made for the OKeh label on 1 October 1928, begins with three reeds wailing a sinister minor-key tune which Miley answers with a fierce plunger-muted obbligato, accompanied by Greer, punctuating a tom-tom pattern with cymbal crashes. The band plays a new theme, and then Bigard plays a solo in the low register of the clarinet. Two outsiders take over and lighten the tone: they are the great blues guitarist

Duke Ellington surrounded by band members in the late 1920s

Lonnie Johnson, and another throaty woman singer, Baby Cox, with a scat vocal. Miley returns, this time with Hodges swooping around him, and the reeds and Miley go back to the theme to end the record in the same mysterious mood it began. 'Hot and Bothered', from the same session, shows the band in quite different form: it is a mad dash, with Hodges and Bigard – neither always able to keep up with the tempo – interrupted by Miley, exchanging phrases with Baby Cox. She was clearly a sexy performer: one shocked reviewer saw her in 'a dance . . . which it is to be hoped will never get to be a ballroom pastime.'⁵¹ Ellington also played, as a piano solo, 'Black Beauty', a piece written to suit Artie Whetsel: when the band as a whole had recorded it the previous March, Whetsel used his delicate muted trumpet to state the wistful theme at a gentle, skipping tempo. The solo record is unusual: until late in his career, Ellington belittled his work as a pianist, calling himself *the piano player in the band* and insisting:

My instrument is the orchestra. In a pioneering piece of critical writing, the British composer and conductor Constant Lambert wrote: 'Ellington himself, being an executant of the second rank, has probably not been tempted to interrupt the continuity of his texture with bravura passages for the piano, and although his instrumentalists are of the highest quality their solos are rarely demonstrations of virtuosity for its own sake.'[52] If this seems a harsh judgement on Ellington's skill as a pianist it is worth remembering that Lambert probably had in mind as first-rank players the likes of Rachmaninov and Rubinstein. Among jazz pianists of Ellington's era, most would feel inadequate, when the competition was headed by Art Tatum (whom even Horowitz regarded with awe) and Earl Hines. So it is not surprising that Duke was a retiring soloist until late in his career. He often started the band from the keyboard, setting the tempo with his introduction – which frequently told the musicians which number they were going to play – and later getting up to conduct and introduce soloists, returning to the piano if needed at the finish. His mastery as a band pianist was complete.

That session at which 'The Mooche' was first recorded was just one of more than 60 which Ellington – using his own name or such pseudonyms as The Jungle Band, The Whoopee Makers or The Memphis Hot Shots – made in recording studios during the years before he left the Cotton Club in February 1931. His contract also allowed him to take up some engagements away from the club, and the famous impresario Florenz Ziegfeld put him on Broadway, in 'Show Girl', a musical comedy with music by George Gershwin and Vincent Youmans, which opened in July, 1929. The Ellington band played on stage in a nightclub scene to end the first act, then headed for the Cotton Club to finish the night. Although the score included the hit 'Liza', the show did poor business and closed in October after the star, Ruby Keeler, dropped out: a few weeks later Ziegfeld's $3,000,000 fortune was wiped out in the Wall Street crash. Around this time Ellington had some *valuable lectures in orchestration*[53] from Ziegfeld's arranger, Will Vodery, who had got him the 'Show Girl' job and was one of the most respected of African-American conductor-composers, along with Will Marion Cook, who gave Ellington advice while riding through New York in taxis. Apart from these informal lessons, Ellington appears to have been self-taught.

By that time Ellington had made a movie. 'Black and Tan', which runs for just under 20 minutes, was shot in a studio at East 24th Street in Manhattan. It gave him an acting as well as a musical role. He plays the lover of the actress Fredi Washington. She has found a club-owner who will give Duke's band work, provided that she dances, in spite of having a heart condition. The band plays three numbers, including 'Black and Tan Fantasy', and Washington dances, collapses and dies when it reaches the funeral march coda. Washington was, in fact, Ellington's lover at the time, and a cause of the break-up of his marriage to Edna, who discovered the affair, waited until Ellington was asleep, and slashed his left cheek with his own knife. Ellington moved out, leaving all his clothes behind.

Ellington and Edna were separated, but never divorced. Interviewed in 1959 at her home in North West Washington, an eleven-room apartment, Edna said: 'Ellington thought I should have been more understanding of him. I guess I should have been. I guess I've regretted – I *know* I've regretted it. You see, I'm still hooked on Ellington.' She added: 'I don't want a divorce and

Fredi Washington (1903–1994) had already acted with Paul Robeson and was to have a distinguished stage and film career, helping to found the Negro Actors Guild. Her first husband was one of Ellington's trombonists, Lawrence Brown, who harboured a resentment against Ellington for his relationship with her and for many years refused to speak to him except at work. She was later divorced from Brown and married a dentist.

neither does he. We're proud of the way we get along. He has always provided for me.'[54] Mercer Ellington believed that his father's determination not to divorce Edna destroyed his affair with Washington, 'one of the most serious relationships of his life',[55] because she realized that they would not be married. About the same time, though, Ellington had an affair with a 'Park Avenue socialite', Mercer said – and soon a Cotton Club dancer, Mildred Dixon, became his lover. In the spring of 1930 Ellington and Mildred moved in together to a seven-room apartment at 381 Edgecombe Avenue, in the prosperous northern part of Harlem called Sugar Hill, where there was space for them, Daisy, J E and Ruth. Mercer spent some of his time there, and some with his mother.

Mildred Dixon 'was petite, with long black hair swept back into a bun, ballerina style. Her finely chiselled features and luminous dark eyes somehow suggested the East Indies. She had innate class comparable to Ellington's own.'[56]

At the end of March that year the Ellington band had returned to Broadway, spending two weeks at the Fulton Street Theatre as part of a vaudeville bill starring the French singer Maurice Chevalier, at which Ellington found that he had to conduct with a baton. In May the band had another two weeks, this time at the Palace Theatre, the pinnacle of variety on Broadway, and Ellington was surprised again: he was expected to announce his numbers. *After, I was praised for my new style of announcing. I have no idea what kind of 'style' it was!*[57] And in August, as part of a tour while the Cotton Club was closed for the summer, the band went to Hollywood to appear in a feature movie. The picture was called 'Check and Double Check', after a catch phrase which all America had learned from the most popular radio show of its time, or perhaps of *all* time, a nightly comic soap-opera called 'Amos 'n' Andy'. The show 'spotlighted two Georgia Negroes whose migration first to Chicago and then to Harlem humorously mirrored the plight of the nation's common man, caught in the transformation from an agrarian society to a complex urban one. The comic currency remained thick dialect speech, malapropisms, and the standard Negro stereotypes: naïveté, imprudence, venality, and ignorance.'[58] Listeners might not have known that the stars were actually Freeman F Golden and Charles J Correl, two white comics: they certainly knew it when they saw them in the movie, covered in burnt-cork make-up (when 'Amos 'n' Andy' moved to televison in 1951, black actors replaced them). The RKO studio bosses were anxious in case the Ellington band looked as though it were a mixture of races, so they blacked-up the lighter-skinned members such as Barney Bigard and Juan Tizol, a recent recruit on valve-trombone. The band perform several Ellington numbers, and others by Harry Ruby and Bert Kalmar, including 'Three Little Words', which appears to be sung by the trumpet-players:

in fact the sound track was made by Bing Crosby and his fellow-members of the Paul Whiteman orchestra's Rhythm Boys, Al Rinker and Harry Barris – they are also on the recording of the song which became Ellington's first No. 1 hit. The trumpets on screen included two new faces, Freddie Jenkins and Cootie Williams. Jenkins is particularly noticeable on film when the brass fan their instruments' bells with derby-hat mutes because he holds his in his right hand while he fingers the valves with his left: a youthful accident had damaged the fingertips of his

Charles 'Cootie' Williams (1910–1985) was born in Mobile, Alabama. He left Ellington in 1940 to join Benny Goodman, then in 1941 formed his own band, making the first record of Thelonious Monk's 'Round Midnight'. He rejoined Ellington in 1962 and stayed until after Duke's death

right hand. Jenkins's hyperactive antics and posturing earned him the nick-name Posey.

Bubber Miley had become unreliable, so Ellington fired him. Cootie Williams said that Bubber was 'the only man he ever fired in his life' because 'every time someone big shot come up to listen to the band there wasn't no Bubber Miley. And he had the whole band built around Bubber Miley.' Although Ellington said nothing to him about it, Williams realized that he was expected to fill Miley's shoes as a plunger and growl specialist. 'I started to play on the plunger . . . by listening to Tricky. I'd go home and rehearse on it.'[59] He added something: 'If he wants to get that savage effect he growls in his throat,' said John Chilton.[60] Williams became one of the most important of the Ellington band's soloists.

Juan Tizol (1900–1984), born in San Juan, Puerto Rico, and a trained musician, spent 15 years with Ellington before joining trumpeter Harry James. He contributed tunes including 'Caravan' and 'Perdido', copied scores and conducted rehearsals. He was also a practical joker.

With Miley no longer able to contribute to compositions, other members of the band helped to make sure that new material was available to excite the Cotton Club customers and sell records outside Harlem. Taking an improvised phrase or counter-melody produced in rehearsal and incorporating it into an existing composition or making it the basis of a new one became an essential feature of Ellington's method. Although some band members complained later that their contributions were not always recognized in the published version of a piece, they often were. So Hodges shared the credit for 'Rent Party Blues', Carney for 'Rockin' in Rhythm', and Whetsel for 'Misty Mornin''. Bigard shared the credit for 'Saturday Night Function' and for the band's big hit: 'Mood Indigo'. 'When I played a solo, or Johnny Hodges played a solo, he'd be listening, and if you made a passage that he liked, he'd write it down and build a tune on it,' Bigard said later. 'All composers borrow from each other. That's nothing new, so long as they don't got too far.'[61] To the composer and critic Gunther Schuller, it was part of Ellington's genius to 'assemble and maintain for over forty years his own private orchestra, comprising musicians more remarkable in their *individuality* than those of any symphony orchestra I know.' Like Haydn, who was able to develop classical symphonic form in daily contact with the Esterhazy orchestra, 'so Ellington practised on his "instrument".'[62] *I like to keep a band so I can write and hear the music next day,* Ellington said. *The only way you can do that is to pay the band and keep it on tap 52 weeks a year.*[63]

'Mood Indigo' began as a piece called 'Dreamy Blues' on a broadcast from the Cotton Club: so many people wrote in about it that Irving Mills had lyrics written for it, giving it the new title. The arrangement reverses the usual New Orleans jazz front line, and gives high notes to Nanton's trombone and the low notes to Bigard's clarinet. Ellington said: *There was a funny sound in the first record we made, and we busted eight more recordings before we found the trouble. There was a loose plunger in the 'mike', and we couldn't get rid of it no how, so what did we do but transpose the piece to another key so the goofy mike sound fitted and it made a swell effect.*[64] 'Mood Indigo' put Ellington among the sheet-music best-sellers: the lyric-writer, Mitchell Parish, was on the publisher's staff, so he did not qualify for royalties. Mills himself was credited as co-composer, and had begun to list himself as lyricist on other numbers. He and Ellington had 45 per cent each of a company called Ellington, Inc., with Mills's lawyer holding 10 per cent: the deal gave Ellington an interest in some other parts of Mills's business. Mills was also publishing Ellington's music, so putting his name on a piece gave him an extra slice of the pie: he claimed that his ideas had contributed to the piece.

Ellington took the view that Mills 's efforts had benefited him in the 20s and 30s, and Mercer wrote: 'There is no point now in debating who profited more from the association, but it' clear that Irving served Ellington well in the formative stages of his career.'[65]

It Don't Mean a Thing
(If it Ain't got That Swing)

At the end of a contract which he had begun to find restrictive, Ellington turned over the stand of the Cotton Club to another bandleader managed by Irving Mill – Cab Calloway, who was about to have a hit with 'Minnie the Moocher' – and set off on the road to meet the public he had won over the radio. Apart from short residencies, including return visits to the Cotton Club for three months at a time, Ellington would be on the road for the next 43 years. Mills, innovative as usual, had *achieved our entry into picture houses, which we pioneered for big bands regardless of race.*[66] An eighteen-week tour of the Paramount-Publix chain, playing between performances of feature movies, began in Boston and moved on to Chicago. The Ellington band did not travel with a specialist singer. The convention of the time was that band members took vocals: the young Bing Crosby, when he was with Paul Whiteman's orchestra, sawed away at a fiddle, conveniently fitted with rubber strings, until it was time for a song. Sonny Greer liked to sing, and the band accompanied vocalists who were part of the Cotton Club shows. But the bosses of the local cinema circuit in Chicago had spotted someone with the band led by the pianist Earl Hines at the Grand Terrace ballroom, and insisted that she join the Ellington band for the month it was to work in the city. Ivie Anderson was chosen over May Alix, a better-known singer who recorded 'Big Butter and Egg Man' with Louis Armstrong, for one reason: Ivie was darker-skinned. Ellington wrote: *In addition to her great singing, Ivie was considered a good-luck charm. We opened at the Oriental Theatre on Friday February 13, 1931, and we broke the all-time house record. We returned to the Oriental on Friday, March 13, 1931, and broke that record, too.*[67] At the end of the fourth week Ellington asked her to stay. It took nearly a year for the band to get back to a recording studio in New York: when it did, Ivie Anderson's first number was prophetic: 'It Don't Mean A Thing (If It Ain't Got That Swing)'. The swing era is often dated to the emergence of the Benny Goodman band in 1935, but Ellington was already swinging.

On 'It Don't Mean a Thing' Anderson scats along with the band's introduction to the song like a jitterbug impatient to get the music moving. She delivers the lyric as a passionate appeal, propaganda for a rhythmic revolution. Yet the voice always had a wistful tinge to it which put her in the first rank of the women singers of the time, comparable with Billie Holiday in expressiveness. At first overawed when she joined Ellington, she relaxed after Sonny Greer developed an act in which he exchanged banter with her, amusing the band as much as the audience with risqué jive talk. 'Our Ivie wasn't a classic beauty, but how lovely she was as she sparkled through every scene, her small, shy smile unexpectedly quickening into an impish bump or dance step,' wrote Rex Stewart. 'When she sang a melancholy refrain such as "Solitude" or "Mood Indigo", oft times the fellows in the band would get caught up in the tide of her emotional portrayal and look sheepishly at each other in wonder at her artistry. The magic of Ivie was in her personality.' Stewart added: 'Off stage our Miss Anderson was another person entirely, bossing the poker game, cussing out Ellington, playing practical jokes or giving some girl-advice about love and life. Then sometimes she would sit very quietly, stoically battling the asthma which took her from us.'[68] Barry Ulanov praised 'her showmanship, her fine understanding of song lyrics and her remarkable feeling for the way this band thought and felt and acted and played.'[69]

Ivie Anderson (1904–1949) was brought up in a convent in California, studied singing in Washington DC and worked on the West Coast and in 'Shuffle Along' before joining Ellington. Later she was in the Marx Brothers' film 'A Day at the Races', singing 'All God's Chillun' Got Rhythm'. She left Ellington in 1942 because of ill health and opened a restaurant.

The big bands which were coming to dominate the music business began to carry singers with them to bring variety to their programmes, and Ivie Anderson was one of the few who travelled with the Ellington band who can be listened to on record with any pleasure. One writer, Robb Holmes, notes that in his memoir, 'Music is my Mistress', Ellington praised a number of singers for their clear enunciation: Holmes argues that he was following precepts of his elementary school principal, Mrs Boston, who *taught us that proper speech and good manners were our first obligations, because as representatives of the Negro race we were to command respect for our people.*[70] Of the men singers Herb Jeffries, who starred in cowboy pictures as 'The Bronze Buckaroo', gave Ellington a hit record with 'Flamingo', and one of his successors, Al Hibbler, had a huge group of fans during and after his time with the band. Of the women, the most musically successful were the guests, from Adelaide Hall at the beginning to the Swedish star Alice Babs at the end. Apart, that is, from Ivie Anderson.

In one of the white gowns she adopted on stage, she scored a sensation in Mills's next break-through, which was to send Ellington abroad for the first time. When the band opened at the London Palladium on 12 June, 1933, *she stopped the show cold,* wrote Ellington. *While she was singing 'Stormy Weather' the audience and all the management brass broke down crying and applauding.*[71]

The visit was recalled by Bert Wilcox, then a 19-year-old earning 15 shillings – 75p – per week, who walked from east London to the Palladium: 'To this day, I can see the flower seller on her regular pitch at the corner of Oxford and Argyll streets and the queue of people in an air of great expectancy. I remember comedian Max Miller finishing his act and suddenly it was Duke and the band in their pearl grey suits, roaring into 'Ring Dem Bells'. It was a moment of sheer magic, but the thing that sticks in my memory is Ivie Anderson leaning against one of the marble pillars and singing "Stormy Weather" without a microphone.'[72]

Professional musicians were also impressed by the band and its recordings. The influential Constant Lambert wrote: 'The scoring and execution of jazz reach a far higher level than that of any previous form of dance music, and in Duke Ellington's compositions jazz has produced the most distinguished popular music since Johann Strauss . . .'[73] Spike Hughes, a composer and critic, told newspaper readers the day before Ellington broadcast nationally on the BBC: 'He is a prophet almost without honour in his own country. To most Americans he is just the successful leader of a successful band which specialises in what are vaguely termed "voodoo harmonies" and "jungle rhythms". It has remained for us in Europe to discover, if not at first hand, at least through the medium of gramophone records, that Duke Ellington is something more than a band-leader: that he is, in fact, the first genuine composer of Jazz.'[74] Ellington's credentials had been recognised the previous year by the Australian composer and piano virtuoso Percy Grainger. Introducing a performance at New York University he made a typically hyperbolic announcement: 'The three greatest composers who ever lived are Bach, Delius and Duke Ellington. Unfortunately Bach is dead, Delius is very ill but we are happy to have with us today The Duke.'[75] Ellington listened to a lot of Delius afterwards, but does not seem to have been influenced by him: there are greater similarities between Ellington and Grainger, whose works are often succinct, based on folk forms, developed through repetition, and employ unusual tone colours.

But Hughes and other critics were disappointed with the 45-minute programme Ellington played at the Palladium, as the closing act of a variety bill, finding it too commercial. At a concert – the first Ellington ever gave---arranged by the music paper 'Melody Maker' at the Trocadero cinema, Elephant and Castle, he started off with his non-commercial pieces, but felt his audience was going to sleep and ended with popular material.

Ellington plays for Percy Grainger (centre) and Irving Mills at NYU in 1932

On a practical level Ellington had run into a problem as soon as the boat-train arrived from Southampton. The 'Daily Express' Music Critic wrote that Ellington was late for a welcoming party because 'There had been some difficulty in finding a London hotel willing – because he is slightly black – to accommodate him.'[76] Ellington was found a room at the Dorchester, but the rest of the band were dispersed around Bloomsbury, where hotels near London University were used to non-white guests. At a party given by Lord Beaverbrook, proprietor of the 'Daily Express', *I fluffed off the guy who kept asking me to play 'Swampy River,' and then found out he was Prince George.*[77] Prince George was the Duke of

Kent, who died in an air crash in 1942, not his brother, the future George VI. Thirty years after the party Ellington told the lyricist Herbert Kretzmer, then a 'Daily Express' writer: *The late Duke of Kent was a pretty fine jazz piano player, did you know that? We played a lot of four-handed duets together. Sometimes the Duke of Windsor sat in, too. He turned out to be a swinging drummer. It wasn't just Little Lord Fauntleroy drumming, I can tell you. The Duke of Windsor had a hell of a Charleston beat.*'[78]

After more than six weeks in Britain, the Ellington band toured briefly in Holland and France and then sailed back to New York. Soon afterwards, an article in 'Fortune', the business magazine which Henry Luce founded as a stable-mate to 'Time', listed the band's achievements and said: 'All of which means that Ellington is a commercial success. Cleverly managed by Irving Mills, he has grossed as much as $250,000 a year, and the band's price for a week's theatre engagement runs as high as $5,500. These figures are, of course, scarcely to be compared to Rudy Vallée's receipts (with a much smaller band he is estimated to have grossed $312,000 in 1931). But what is remarkable is that Ellington has never compromised with the public taste for watery popular songs, for "show bands" combining music with scenic effects, low comedy and flag drills. He has played *hot* music, his own music, all the way along.'[79] Meanwhile Rudy Vallée, having started with a megaphone, was radiating charm behind the microphone while crooning 'Life Is Just A Bowl Of Cherries' and 'I'm a Dreamer, Aren't We All?' to the country-club crowd.

Ellington had scored another break-through by making the first double-sided popular record and his first extended composition, 'Creole Rhapsody'. The first version took two sides of a 10-inch 78, the second, with changes in tempo and mood, took both sides of a 12-inch 78. It was not likely to be a big seller, but in 1932 Ellington recorded 'Solitude', one of his most successful ballads. It won a $2,500 prize for the best popular song of the year from the performing rights organisation, the American Society of Composers, Authors and Publishers – membership of which Mills got for Ellington in 1935, the year he wrote 'In a Sentimental Mood.' An instrumental piece, 'Rude Interlude', got its title because Constant Lambert's wife, Florence Kaye, misheard Duke's introduction of 'Mood Indigo', and thought he had said '*Rude* Indigo'.

During the Depression years, Ellington's band toured the United States in comparative comfort, avoiding the routine humiliations and the dingy accommodation to which black travellers were often relegated, because Ellington and Mills had hired two Pullman carriages so that the entourage could not simply travel but sleep undisturbed. Rex Stewart remembered: 'Joining the Ellington entourage meant travel by Pullman and a decent bed to sleep in every night, even if frequently this was just our usual Pullman berth on the railway siding.'[80] The Ellington carriages, plus a baggage wagon, would be hitched on to a train to go from city to city, and then parked in a siding while the band played its date.

Each time the train had to be loaded: 'Sonny Greer had six huge trunks for his clothes, timpani, cymbals, vibraphone and drums. Ivie carried three trunks, one each for stage gowns and street clothes and a special trunk for coats and shoes. Then there were the trunks for scenery and the light console. The microphone and sound system were in separate trunks. This was only the beginning. Still to come would be the three uniform trunks, the shirt trunk, instrument trunks, plus the personal trunk of each fellow. Duke also carried five personal trunks and an especially made trunk for his shoes! Oh, I almost forgot the music stand trunk and the trunks for music.'[81] Once the train left the siding there was poker, with hundreds of dollars changing hands, usually in two games, one with unlimited stakes and the other with a 25-dollar maximum. 'They called the first the Big Top and the small game the Side Show,' Stewart recalled. 'Duke and Ivie Anderson were the rulers of the Big Top; they not only had card sense and skill, they also had the money to make a faint-hearted player turn down the best hands when they decided to put the old pressure on. The Side Show was the bailiwick of the unholy twins, as we called Sony Greer and Otto Hardwick.'[82]

Duke's orchestra continued to appear in films throughout the 1930s. The historian of popular music, Dr Sigmund Spaeth, wrote: 'There is a true story of Duke Ellington's appearance at a movie studio to make a short picture with his band. They arrived without a single note of music and merely asked for a half hour of rehearsal time, during which they worked out a ten-minute routine, completely created on the spot, including even the melodic materials. Such a performance must be considered in the true tradition of New Orleans jazz.'[83] In 1934 the band was in Hollywood for 'Murder at the Vanities', a backstage mystery which gave Ellington a No. 1 hit record with 'Cocktails for Two,' by Arthur Johnston and Sam Coslow, and for a Mae West feature which started out as 'It Ain't No Sin' and wound up being called

Billie Holiday in 'Symphony in Black', filmed in 1934

'Belle of the Nineties'. Later in the year, for a ten-minute short made at the Astoria Studio in Queens, New York – where the movie 'Cotton Club' was shot in the 1980s – Ellington assembled one new piece and three old ones into a 'Symphony in Black'. A sinister blues, 'The Saddest Tale', was given new lyrics and sung by Billie Holiday, then just being discovered. In March 1937 the band was in 'The Hit Parade', a feature with a show-business plot providing an excuse for songs. Ivie Anderson sang an up-tempo number gently mocking the jitterbugs, 'I've Got To Be a Rug-Cutter,' helped by a vocal trio and some stamping feet from the band. Then, on a sound stage at Republic Pictures, Duke himself sat alone at the piano and made a demo recording of the song, hinting at Ivie's scat-singing asides. His tone is amused and conversational, but his voice is oddly colourless: the recording went unissued until many years later, and, although Ellington was never reluctant to speak on stage or on record – notably on 'The Saddest Tale' in 1934 and the urban fairy-tale 'Monologue' in 1951 – this seems to be the only time he sang for the micro-phone apart from tentative versions of two of his current pop songs made in his hotel room in Detroit in 1950.

The band continued to evolve, keeping up with the trend to fleeter, less emphatic rhythm. Fred Guy used the voyage to Europe to convert from the four-string banjo to the six-string guitar, bringing a more modern sound to the rhythm section. Braud was joined by a second bass-player, Billy Taylor, and quit: it may be that Ellington found his slapped-bass technique old-fashioned, and was trying to push him out. But he hired another bassist, Hayes Alvis, and continued to work with two. Toby Hardwick returned, bringing the reeds up to four and strength-ening the lower tones when he used his bass saxophone alongside or instead of Carney's baritone. Two important new soloists came into the band: Lawrence Brown brought the trombones up to three, and Rex Stewart replaced Freddie Jenkins. Brown represented a new kind of trombonist with a formidable technique, a player similar to Jack Teagarden or Tommy Dorsey. In contrast to the idiosyncratic 'primitive' outbursts of Nanton, Brown produced cello-like sounds and a legato line. Ellington wrote the astonishing 'Braggin' in Brass' to show off his virtuoso trombone section. Stewart, who played the warmer-toned cornet rather than trumpet, developed a series of 'talking' effects, some by holding the valves half-way down, some by relaxing his embouchure to create rasping noises at the bottom of the instrument's range. On a visit to London John Chilton got a lesson from him on half-valving and found that Stewart had an encyclopaedic knowledge of

Rex Stewart (1907–1967) spent eight years with Ellington. Later he turned to writing memoirs and jazz criticism

Lawrence Brown (1907–1988) was with Ellington from 1932 to 1951, rejoined in 1960 and stayed until 1970, when he stopped playing.

which fingerings would work and which would not: 'It's so complicated – he must have spent thousands of hours practising.'[84]

Stewart was the first member involved in a new initiative, to make records by small groups drawn from the band for release on Variety, a 35-cent cut-price label owned by Irving Mills. His group got the name of Rex Stewart and his 52nd Street Stompers, but all but one of the eight players came from Ellington's band, including Duke on the piano. Stewart was followed by Barney Bigard and his Jazzopaters, Cootie Williams and his Rug Cutters and Johnny Hodges and His Orchestra. At a time when the depression had sharply reduced record sales, the small-group sides were cheaper to make as well as to buy. They were supervised by Helen Oakley, a society girl from Toronto who had been in London for Ellington's visit there and would later marry Stanley Dance, an English-born critic and supporter of Ellington. Other small group swing sessions were on rival labels: leaders included Benny Goodman, Lionel Hampton and John Kirby. Ellington and his men seem especially relaxed, and Greer seems happier, effortlessly swinging the small group though he often sounded overworked when he had to propel the full band. From Ellington, who is on most of the records, the small groups stimulated some of his finest compositions, such as 'Dooji Wooji', 'Wanderlust' and 'The Boys from Harlem'. Meanwhile, for Mills's Master label, at the full price of 70 cents, Ellington recorded 'Caravan', with Tizol as co-composer and soloist, and scored a hit. Tizol sold the tune outright to Irving Mills for $25. 'Later on he decided to give me a percentage, and thank God, at least I got something from "Caravan",' said Tizol.[85]

Most jazz has the quality of 'swing', the result of a steady pulse going on at the same time as one or more counter-rhythms, creating tension for the listener. The word came to mean the big-band music popular and highly publicised in the 30s. In a 1939 article Ellington declared that musicians who had been swinging 10 or 15 years before *today look on, some with amusement, others with intolerance, at the farce which is being played out to the full on that merry-go-round known as the amusement world.*[86]

This creative period for Ellington began in 1936, after he had recovered from a shattering personal blow. In 1934 Daisy Ellington was found to be suffering from cancer. She went to Detroit for treatment, but died there on 27 May, 1935: Ellington and other members of the family were there. With the death of the woman who told him he was 'blessed', Ellington fell into a depression. 'He had always felt that he and his activities were the special concern of a benevolent God. In the face of this tragedy, he began

J E Ellington, Duke and Ivie Anderson at a station in 1936

to doubt it,' wrote a 'New Yorker' writer. 'It was then that he began wearing the little gold cross that always hangs around his neck. He read his Bible through three times in 1935 in an effort to regain his equilibrium.'[87] Ellington's brooding over his mother's death produced his longest work to that date, 'Reminiscing in Tempo', which was recorded on four 10-inch sides, an unprecedented length for a popular-music piece. It was immediately attacked by John Hammond, a jazz journalist with influence in America and Britain, as 'formless and shallow',[88] but more recently the composer Gunther Schuller praised its 'compositional craft and structural unity'[89] during a close musical analysis.

J E Ellington, who had become a heavy drinker, tried to dry out and failed. In 1937 he went into a New York hospital with pleurisy, and died on 28 October. The bills for his parents' treatment had put Ellington in debt, but his situation improved when he had a long engagement at the Cotton Club, which had left Harlem behind and moved to 200 West 48th, near Broadway. It was at the new Cotton Club that he met Arthur Logan, who became his doctor and also his closest friend. 'They had a unique, incredible, unexplainable friendship,' said Logan's wife, Marian.[90] For the next 37 years the Logans' phone might ring at any time and Ellington would ask, from wherever in the world his tours had taken him, *How do I feel today?* Before performances Logan would sometimes give him injections: Ellington believed they were multi-vitamin shots, but Logan told a friend that they were often water.

Also at the Cotton Club he met Beatrice Ellis, known as Evie, 'a beautiful woman among a lot of beautiful women,'[91] said Mercer, 'not a chorus girl, but one of those who walked and stood around and posed in beautiful gowns.' Ellington moved in with her on St Nicholas Place, again leaving all his clothes behind at his old apartment. They moved to 935 St Nicholas

Avenue and then to 400 Central Park West, near 100th Street. Until Ellington's death they lived at 140 West End Avenue and 66th Street, a few blocks from the Lincoln Centre arts complex and with a view from the twenty-second floor of the Hudson River – their names were on the door as Bea Ellis and Edward K Ellington. Mercer and Ruth, left behind in Edgecombe Avenue with Mil Dixon, realized that their father would never return, even for a visit. So they moved a little way uptown to 409 Edgecombe, leaving the furniture with Mil. Ruth went to Paris in the summer of 1938, to study languages at the Sorbonne. Ellington sent a chaperon with her.

There was a business upheaval, too. Ellington examined Mills's books and ended the partnership: one version of the story says that Ellington had wanted Daisy buried in a $5,000-dollar coffin, but Mills had bought a cheaper one. Ellington gave back the shares he held in Mills's company in exchange for Mills's shares in Ellington, Inc. The William Morris Agency became Ellington's booking agent, Jack Robbins became his publisher instead of Mills Music. The Master and Variety labels had been taken over by Columbia, and for one label or another Ellington had produced a string of Top Ten hits through the Thirties. They included 'Merry-go-Round', 'Oh Babe! Maybe Someday', 'Caravan' and in the spring of 1938 his third No. 1, an instrumental version of 'I Let a Song Go Out of My Heart.' But in 1939 new owners put John Hammond in charge of Columbia jazz recordings. Ellington, perhaps thinking back to 'Reminiscing in Tempo', complained publicly that Hammond had a conflict

'Evie was a grade-A, stand-up, loyal lady . . . No matter what happened he knew he could count on her. He had put her through every test. He had cheated on her, neglected her and put her through the wringer like no other woman. But she was always there when he needed her.'

Don George[92]

of interest as being at the same time critic and producer, and went to Victor, with a deal that promised him he would be the only black band on the full-price 75-cent label. He was about to reach what most of his admirers think of as the peak of his career.

Take the 'A' Train

Early in December 1938, Duke Ellington met the man who would become his musical collaborator in an intimate and long-lasting partnership. Between shows at the Stanley Theatre in Pittsburgh, Billy Strayhorn, a pianist who was earning a living as a drugstore soda-jerk and delivery boy, came to his dressing-room. While Ellington's valet did his hair, Strayhorn played 'Sophisticated Lady', at first imitating the way Ellington had played it on stage, and then in his own style. Impressed, Ellington gave him an idea for a lyric and asked him to work on it. Strayhorn came back with it the next night. Later in the week he completed an arrangement of 'Two Sleepy People', the hit song from a new Bob Hope film. The band performed it with Ivie Anderson during one of its shows; Ellington paid Strayhorn $20 for it and wrote out directions for him to reach Edgecombe Avenue by subway, although he was not certain how he could be fitted into the organisation.

Strayhorn moved into 409 Edgecombe Avenue. For a Johnny Hodges small-group recording session, Ellington gave him two pieces to arrange, and he had to work overnight to complete them, falling asleep on the kitchen table and carrying on working when he woke up again. The results, on 'Savoy Strut' and 'Like a Ship in the Night', were enough to persuade Ellington, who played the piano on the session, to hand over almost all the small-group recordings to Strayhorn. Then, on March 21, 1939, the Duke Ellington orchestra recorded its first Strayhorn composition, 'Something to Live For,' though with Ellington credited as co-composer. Jean Eldridge, a singer who spent a year with Ellington's

Billy Strayhorn (1915–1967) was born in Dayton, Ohio, and brought up in Pittsburgh. He was classically-trained as a pianist and wrote songs and shows for local performance. His music and lyrics for a sophisticated cabaret song, 'Lush Life', were completed about 1936, although it was not recorded until 1948, as part of an Ellington concert at Carnegie Hall. 'He was only about 5 feet 1 inch tall and occasionally looked like a small, slightly- burned whole-wheat-toast owl'[93]

band alongside Ivie Anderson, gave Strayhorn's lyric the appropriate yearning note. Two days later, Ellington took the band for a tour of Europe, mainly in Sweden. In the seven weeks while they were away, Strayhorn got out some of Ellington's scores to study his methods, as well as writing new works of his own, including the instrumental ballads 'Day Dream' and 'Passion Flower', which would soon be recorded by Hodges small groups as the first of similar Strayhorn showpieces for the alto saxophonist throughout his career. He was put in charge of arrangements for singers and pressed into service as a stand-in pianist. The collaboration with Ellington developed over the years so that, as Gunther Schuller wrote, 'the match is so close that it is frequently impossible to tell with certainty where the work of one ends and the other's begins.'[94] Later in the year Ellington would give a hint at the place Strayhorn had won in the organisation by recording a musical portrait of him under the title 'Weely', Strayhorn's original nickname in the band, a version of Willie. He soon became 'Swee' Pea', because he reminded Toby Hardwick, who took charge of handing out nicknames, of the baby in the Popeye cartoons. Or simply 'Strays'.

Looking out of the apartment window one day, Mercer Ellington spotted a young neighbour, Aaron Bridgers, who had a job as a lift operator in an hotel while he studied the piano. He took Strayhorn down to introduce him, knowing that both young men were lonely and didn't know many people in New York. 'We had everything in common, particularly music,' Bridgers said.

He was not, as he was often referred to by many, my alter ego. Billy Strayhorn was my right arm, my left arm, all the eyes in the back of my head, my brain waves in his head, and his in mine.[95]

'We became very close right away.'[96] Both Strayhorn and Bridgers were gay, and they soon moved in together to an apartment on Convent Avenue in Sugar Hill. 'Pop never cared one bit that

Strayhorn was gay,' said Mercer. 'He had been exposed to homosexuality his whole life in the music business. It was nothing new to him . . . He backed up Strayhorn all the way.'[97]

Strayhorn's value as an associate became crucial in March 1940, when ASCAP demanded an increase in the licensing fee for broadcasts of its members' music. The radio stations refused, and set up a rival licensing company, BMI – Broadcast Music Incorporated. Music by ASCAP members vanished from the air, and so did broadcast royalties to composers like Ellington. But Strayhorn and Mercer Ellington were not ASCAP members, and they set to work to provide the band with a new book for broadcasting – Mercer gave up a big band he had been leading for a year, without much success, to help with the family business. His contributions included 'Moon Mist', 'Blue Serge' and 'Things Ain't What They Used To Be.' Strayhorn wrote, among others, 'After All', 'Chelsea Bridge' – and 'Take the "A" Train', named after the Eighth Avenue express subway service which goes through Harlem. Strayhorn told a friend that the piece was based on Ellington's note on how to get to his apartment, and was written in 1939, but that he feared the style was too much like that of Ellington's rival bandleader, Fletcher Henderson, whose arrangements were by that time at the heart of the success of the Benny Goodman band. In 1941, though, with his former signature tune banned from the air by the ASCAP-BMI dispute, Ellington chose 'Take the "A" Train' to replace it, and used it after the dispute was resolved in 1941, and for the rest of his life. Don George, the lyric-writer, watched Ellington and Strayhorn at work, and wrote that many pieces 'were written with Duke doing part, then handing it to Sweetpea, saying, 'Here, man, you finish it.' . . . They had gotten into each other's minds and musical areas so completely that when it came to anybody being able to discern who wrote what, very often they themselves didn't know what part each had written.'[98]

As the 1940s were about to begin, Ellington's band consisted of mature musicians in their thirties, the core of which had been playing together almost every day for a decade. Two additions to this remarkable group gave it a new drive, and Ellington's imagination a new stimulus. The first was Jimmie Blanton, a young man who revolutionised jazz bass-playing. He was 19 years old when Duke Ellington's band came to St Louis, Missouri, for a two-week residency at the Hotel Coronado's nightclub, the first black band to play there. Blanton was at the Club 49, an after-hours joint, playing in a band led by Fate Marable, a veteran musician who had employed Louis Armstrong in orchestras on Mississippi riverboats at the start of the 1920s. Several members of the Ellington band claimed to have alerted Duke to Blanton and the local African-American newspaper noted: 'Duke Ellington has been frequenting Club 49 these nites in town. We wonder if the maestro is planning to add Jimmie Blanton, bass fiddler with Fate Marable's band, to his aggregation.'[100] He was: Blanton left with the band at the end of the engagement on 2 November, making a second bass-player with Billy Taylor. A month later, in Indianapolis, 'Jimmie Blanton really played the bass fiddle and was featured before the mike on that unforgettable 'Sophisticated Lady', wrote a columnist calling himself Ye Scribe. 'It was really unique and fascinating and spine-chilling.'[101] A month after that, at the Southland Café in Boston, *Right in the middle of a set, Billy Taylor*

'Ellington plays the piano, but his real instrument is the band. Each member of his band is to him a distinctive tone color and set of emotions, which he mixes with others equally distinctive to produce a third thing, which I like to call the Ellington Effect. Sometimes the mixing happens on paper and frequently right on the bandstand. I have often seen him exchange parts in the middle of a piece because the man and the part weren't the same character.

Billy Strayhorn[99]

Jimmie Blanton (1918–1942) was born in Chattanooga, Tennessee. *He played melodies that belonged to the bass and always had a foundation quality. Rhythmically, he supported and drove at the same time. He was just too much.*[103]

picked up his bass and said, 'I'm not going to stand up here next to that young boy playing all that bass and be embarrassed'[102]

While an earlier generation of jazz bass-players had started on tuba, and tended to imitate its phrasing, Blanton's first instrument had been the violin, and that may go some way to explain his facility in fingering, which was unprecedented, or the rich, sustained tone he got out of a plucked bass in a period long before the use of amplifiers. Ellington made two sessions of duets with Blanton, in which the bass is the soloist and the piano accompanies it. The two sides for Columbia are dimly recorded in comparison with the four for Ellington's new label, Victor, including 'Pitter Panther Patter' and 'Mr J B Blues'. The Victor engineers capture the variety of Blanton's tone as well as its breadth. And the same is true of the series of recordings the complete band embarked on in 1940.

Another reason why the band sounds so much fuller is that Ellington had hired a fifth reed player, the tenor saxophonist Ben Webster. Although Bigard played tenor in the section, he did not solo; Carney took baritone solos in the tradition of the tenor pioneer, Coleman Hawkins. But the other swing bands had made tenor saxophones into star instruments: Andy Kirk had Dick Wilson, Jimmie Lunceford had Joe Thomas, Count Basie had two, Lester Young and Buddy Tate. Webster came from Kansas City, Missouri, known to be a breeding-ground of aggressive tenor-players, and he proved that for Ellington on 'Cottontail'; but he could also pour out streams of breathy tone for sexy ballads like 'All Too Soon'. On top of that, wrote Ellington, *his enthusiasm and drive had an especially important influence o the saxophone section.*[104]

In ensembles, Mercer Ellington explained, the four established players complained if Webster, playing by ear, doubled a note one of them was used to playing. 'So Ben decided he would get away from this and find a note nobody had. What was a four-part reed chorus in four-part harmony suddenly had five parts – in self-defence, along with great musicianship, by Ben.'[105] Ellington, said Mercer, soon learned to use the device in his scores.

Ben Webster (1909–1973), known as 'Frog' or 'The Brute', freelanced as a soloist after leaving Ellington, spending the 1950s in California to look after his mother. He moved to Copenhagen in 1964 and was a favourite visitor to Ronnie Scott's Club in London, where staff and fans became wary of his temper when drunk. Sober, he was polite and friendly.

The three new recruits to the band, its youngest members, quickly formed an alliance. Blanton was 'worried about making good with the greatest of all bands,' wrote Barry Ulanov. 'Billy helped him over some of the first hesitancies, the rough moments inevitable in any man's first days with a social unit as tight as a dance band.' Webster was also protective of the fragile-looking Blanton, whom he nicknamed 'Bear'. The first Victor session shows the difference Blanton made: to introduce 'Jack the Bear' Ellington gives him a solo. It would be unthinkable for any earlier bass-player to be so exposed in a big band, except as an elephantine joke. Ellington's listeners at the time would have been astonished at the novelty: after more than half a century of hard work in which bassists have achieved amazing dexterity, there are few who have been able to equal the power and beauty of Blanton's work. He has a vital role in the number that followed in the studio, 'Ko-Ko', a threatening minor-key blues, the pinnacle of the jungle style with one of Nanton's most savage solos, and a few days later in 'Concerto for Cootie', in which, naturally, Williams is the main soloist. In these and the string of Ellington masterpieces which followed, the rhythm section has acquired a new lightness and flexibility at every tempo, ranging from 'Me and You', in which one of Ivie Anderson's most joyful vocals leads to a stomping climax with solos by Lawrence Brown and Johnny Hodges, to 'Dusk', which has Rex Stewart half-valving in a twilight nostalgic tone-poem. The same burst of creativity produced two of Ellington's most enduring songs, 'All Too Soon' and 'Never No Lament' – 'Don't Get Around Much Anymore' when it had been given a lyric, bringing in $22,500 in a single royalty cheque. The opening of 'Concerto for Cootie' was transformed into 'Do Nothin' Till You Hear From Me.'

As for 'Harlem Air Shaft', one of his most exciting instrumental pieces, Ellington famously provided what concert composers would call a 'programme' for it: *You get the full essence of Harlem in an air shaft. You hear fights, you smell dinner, you hear people making love. You hear intimate gossip floating down. You hear the radio. An air shaft is one great big loudspeaker. You see your neighbour's laundry. You hear the janitor's dogs* . . . and so on, until . . . *Jitterbugs are jumping up and down always over you, never below you. That's a funny thing about jitterbugs. They're always above you. I tried to put all that in 'Harlem Air Shaft'.*[106] It seems accurate as we listen to the record, except that Victor mixed up the sides recorded that day: what was issued as 'Harlem Air Shaft' was originally written as 'Rumpus in Richmond', a reference to the sedate fifth borough of New York, usually known as Staten Island. The piece released as 'Rumpus in Richmond' was originally titled 'Brassiere'. Probably Ellington, like most improvising composers, wrote pieces first and found titles afterwards.

The studio records Ellington made in 1940 are classics of jazz, and they capture the band in virtuosic form. But we get a more accurate idea of what it was like to be at an Ellington performance from the results of an evening's work by two young enthusiasts who were at the Crystal Ballroom in Fargo, North Dakota, on 7 November that year. Jack Towers and Dick Burris brought in a disc-cutter and three microphones to record two hours of music, playing back parts of it to some of the musicians during intervals. The sound is, naturally, imperfect, and some numbers are incomplete, but the recording shows the enthusiasm and vigour with which the band could perform, perhaps inspired by the presence of dancers enjoying themselves. It also demonstrates that many of the performances went on for longer than the standard three minutes of a 10-inch 78: 'Pussy Willow', for example, at four and a half minutes, has a more meaningful shape. Ivie Anderson sings two songs she did not record otherwise, with arrangements which sound as though they were by Strayhorn, suggesting how repertoire had to vary to take notice of fashion: although it seems improbable now, one of them, 'Ferryboat Serenade', was one of 1940's hit tunes. The band also shows how it can adapt to changing circumstances by accompanying the trumpeter Ray Nance in a vocal for which they are unlikely to have had an arrangement. Nance was a new member: the Ellington scholar Roger Boyes thinks it likely that he joined only the day before, in Winnipeg. Cootie Williams had left four days earlier to get a pay rise reputed to be $25 a week: 'All white musicians in name bands earned more than we did and Cootie would move into the white pay schedule with Benny Goodman,' wrote Rex Stewart.[107]

In 1941 Ellington was working in Los Angeles and playing

Ray Nance (1913–1976) a Chicagoan, played trumpet and violin, sang, danced and did comedy routines. He got the nickname 'Floorshow'

in a jam session at the home of a screenwriter, Sid Kuller, who said: '"The joint sure is jumpin'."' Duke turned and said, *Jumpin' for joy.* I said: "That's it, why don't we do a show with Ellington,

'Jump for Joy'?"[108] Left-wing writers and actors in Hollywood raised the money and the show, a series of songs and sketches advertised as 'A Sun-Tanned Revue-sical', opened at the Mayan Theatre on 10 July, with music by Ellington and Hal Borne, lyrics by Paul Francis Webster and Kuller, and contributions by Strayhorn, Mercer Ellington, Langston Hughes and Mickey Rooney, among others. In the cast were the young Dorothy Dandridge, later to be 'Carmen Jones', Ivie Anderson, Herb Jeffries and the Kansas City blues shouter Joe Turner. The Ellington band was in the pit. The aim was to clear away theatrical stereotypes about African-Americans, celebrate instead genuine black humour and culture, including contemporary phenomena such as 'the zoot suit with a drape shape and a reet pleat.' Ivie sang the hit, 'I Got it Bad (and That Ain't Good)' and other numbers had a direct social point: 'I've Got a Passport from Georgia (and I'm Sailing for the USA)' and 'Uncle Tom's Cabin is a Drive-In Now'. The show gave Ellington an opportunity to express some of his thoughts and feelings on the history and status of African-Americans. But it ran only 101 performances, closing on 27 September without a chance of the Broadway transfer Ellington longed for. Barry Ulanov wrote: 'It left enough of an impression so that most of those who saw it and are concerned with a vigorous and honest Negro theatre continually refer to it as *the* Negro musical. It was probably the only employment of coloured singers and dancers and comedians which really didn't lapse into crude caricature of the Negro at some point, which didn't pander to the white man's distorted idea. . . it was ahead of its time and presented on the wrong coast of America for theatrical success, but it made its valorous point.' Orson Welles put Ellington on a $1,000-per-week retainer to work on a history of jazz for a feature called 'It's All True'. It was never completed, but Ellington earned $12,500 for doing very little, and an idea was planted in his mind.

Duke Ellington jamming with friends – Johnny Hodges on the far right

While the band was in Los Angeles Jimmie Blanton became increasingly ill with tuberculosis, and a second bassist, Alvin 'Junior' Raglin, joined the band. When the band returned to touring, Blanton was left behind. The Cab Calloway band had arrived in town, and Ben Webster talked to its bassist, Milt Hinton: 'Ben said to me, "Bear's pretty sick. We gotta leave him in a rest home here. Please go out and see him."' Hinton went every other day to see Blanton, who was suffering from a disease for which the only cure at the time was bed rest. After the band left, Hinton said, 'His poor heart was broken. You could see the loneliness of it took his strength and will to live.'[109] Blanton died on 30 July, 1942. When the news reached the band, at the Hotel Sherman in Chicago, Webster cried so hard that he had to leave the stand. A few days later Ivie Anderson quit the band to open a restaurant, Ivie's Chicken Shack, off Central Avenue in Los Angeles: she was to die in 1949, of the effects of asthma. The band had already lost Herb Jeffries and Barney Bigard, both of whom had decided to stay in California.

Payroll sheets for a week at the end of January, 1942, when the band was at a Chicago movie theatre, the Oriental, show that Ellington was paid $250 and Stewart was the highest-paid sideman at $135. Bigard, Carney, Hodges and Tizol got $130 each, Ivie Anderson and Greer $125 and most of the rest $105. Junior Raglan, the new bassist, was paid $80 and Billy Strayhorn $75. For the session on 21 January which produced four sides, including 'Perdido' and 'C Jam Blues', the sidemen's fees were $30 each, except for Hodges, who was paid $50.[110]

Before he left, 'Barney wasn't speaking to Lawrence Brown, who was not on speaking terms with Ellington,'[111]wrote Rex Stewart, who did not speak to Cootie Williams, in the next chair, for two years. Working conditions deteriorated: even before the United States entered the Second World War in December 1941 the musicians noticed 'an almost imperceptible tightening of the nation's economic belt,' according to Stewart, with fewer dates, longer lay-offs and travel in ordinary railway carriages instead of Pullmans.[112]

Christmas bonuses to musicians vanished, and from August 1942 they lost income because the American Federation of Musicians banned recording, claiming that it reduced audiences for live music, and demanding that record companies pay into a fund for unemployed players. Victor did not settle with the union until December 1944, so there are no commercial recordings of the Ellington band for nearly 18 months.

In need of a lead trumpet in September 1942, Ellington had hired Harold 'Shorty' Baker away from a six-piece band he was leading with the pianist Mary Lou Williams, his lover and a former lover of Ben Webster. Without Baker, a fine soloist as well as a superb section player, the little band limped along for a while, and then Williams decided to travel with Baker: they were married in Baltimore in December. The result was that Ellington had at hand a great arranger, who had provided the core of the book for Andy Kirk and his Clouds of Joy, in which she was the star

Mary Lou Williams 1957 – Chuck Stewart

soloist, and a jazz composer of real stature: Williams later wrote an ambitious twelve-movement 'Zodiac Suite' and, after becoming a devout Roman Catholic, large-scale sacred works. 'Duke asked me to write some arrangements. I told him: "What in the world am I going to write for you?"'[113] Among other pieces, she wrote arrangements of standards such as Hoagy Carmichael's 'Star Dust' and Irving Berlin's 'Blue Skies'---a spectacular display piece for his trumpet section, re-titled 'Trumpets All Out', which Ellington frequently used to end concerts for ten years. *Mary Lou Williams is perpetually contemporary,* Ellington wrote. *She is like soul on soul.*[114] According to the archivist Annie Kuebler, who has an expert knowledge of the Ellington music manuscripts and Williams's archive, she provided 15 or 16 pieces as a staff arranger and five or six as a freelance afterwards. In 1967 four of her compositions appeared uncredited in Ellington's ballet 'The River'. In the 1930s Ellington had swapped scores with the Casa Loma Orchestra, a popular white band, and even when the crisis caused by the ASCAP dispute was over, Ellington used arrangers from outside his organisation, often to provide arrangements of current pop songs which might be requested by audiences. They included the trumpeters Dick Vance and Gerald Wilson and band members such as the saxophonist Norris Turney and the trombonist Vince Prudente. Sessions in 1962 and 1963 for a project called 'Will the Big Bands Ever Come back?', which used the theme songs of rival bands (most of them disbanded), borrowed the original arrangements in some cases.[115]

I don't write jazz. I write Negro folk music.[116]

Ellington had been planning a major work about black history, described at different times as an opera, a symphony, a suite or a musical. One possible name for it was 'Boola'. The opportunity for a premiere of a piece which would not primarily be dance music came when his manager, William Morris, arranged for him to give a concert at Carnegie Hall in New York.

For six weeks Ellington worked to produce 'Black, Brown and Beige', sub-titled 'A Tone Parallel to the History of the American Negro,' which would occupy nearly fifty minutes of a three-hour concert. The three sections follow African-Americans through slavery and devotion to religion ('Black'), involvement in the War of Independence and the Civil War leading to Emancipation ('Brown') and into the 20th century ('Beige'). Each section is in several movements, and the only aspect of the piece which listeners have agreed on since its official premiere on 23 January, 1943, is that it is uneven. The absence of a formal structure that might be expected in classical music annoyed some critics; others lamented the absence of dance rhythms in some sections. The specialist jazz press was full of praise. It was played in full only twice more, within the next six weeks, at concerts in Boston and Cleveland. People who could not be there had to be satisfied with excerpts on four 12inch sides made when the recording ban ended. Acetates made on the night later became available, but the sound is poor, and a clearer idea of the work can be got from the reconstruction made by Brian Priestley and Alan Cohen and played by London musicians under Cohen's leadership in 1972.

Although the critical reception was discouraging, Ellington continued to write extended works – none so ambitious as 'Black, Brown and Beige' – and present them in six more concerts at Carnegie Hall in the next few years. In December 1943 he played 'New World A-Comin'', an optimistic reflection on the African-American future with an important solo piano part, and there followed 'The Perfume Suite', 'A Tonal Group', 'Liberian Suite' and 'The Tattooed Bride'. The December 1943 concert also saw the introduction of an element that was to recur in many of his appearances: the medley. This pot-pourri of truncated versions of various compositions from the past exasperated serious audiences, but it satisfied requests and left time for more recent pieces. Mercer explained that it was also profitable: 'When it comes to

ASCAP, you get so much for the numbers you perform, he had enough in there for them to be counted as performances, and so in ten minutes he had twenty tunes he had performed that he would get the dough for.'[117]

Soon after Ellington's Carnegie Hall debut he went into his first New York nightclub residency for five years, at the Hurricane, at 51st Street and Broadway. He was booked for six weeks and stayed for six months, making spectacular entrances playing an upright piano on a platform lowered from the ceiling. Rex Stewart described the way Ellington presented himself on stage at the height of his career: 'Once he had a black satin jacket enhanced by a weskit of the same material, which he wore with houndstoooth slacks and black suede quaker-type shoes complete with silver buckles. And another exotic outfit was the peach-coloured lounge coat with a tie of the same colour over a chartreuse shirt and pearl grey sacks, with shoes to match.'[118] Rehearsing or composing, though, 'he likes to wear a cheap hat, the brim turned up all around, a sports shirt without a tie, the points of the collar long enough to reach almost to his chest, brown suède shoes, a blue or maroon pullover sweater, and a sports coat so tailored it makes him look slender.'[119] 'He felt that green was bad luck,' said Mercer. 'He didn't like yellow either. He never said too much about red, but he didn't like black or grey. He had a thing about brown because he was wearing a brown suit the day his mother died . . . he dressed almost entirely in blue whenever he could, right down to his shoes.'[120] He would not wear binding things, according to Don George: 'He never wore a wristwatch or a belt or shoelaces. He hated ties, and when he had to wear one he wore a big, high-collared, soft shirt so he wouldn't feel them.'[121] Between shows he put on a cotton bathrobe and kept his hair in place with an old silk stocking.

At 6 ft. 1 in., Ellington looked plump and was trying to diet, ordering cereal, saying grace over it, and then seeing others' meals and calling for a steak. 'Then he really begins to eat. He has another steak, smothered in onions, a double portion of fried potatoes, a salad, a bowl of sliced tomatoes, a giant lobster and melted butter, coffee, and an Ellington dessert – perhaps a combination of pie, cake, ice cream, custard, pastry, jello, fruit and cheese. His appetite really whetted, he may order ham and eggs, a half-dozen pancakes, waffles and syrup, and some hot biscuits. Then, determined to get back on his diet, he will finish, as he began, with Shredded Wheat and black tea.'[123] In later years he lost weight and lived on steak, grapefruit, salad and ice cream. He stopped drinking heavily about 1940 and had virtually given up alcohol by the 1960s: *I retired undefeated champ.*[124] He drank coffee with lemon, weak tea, hot water, or glass after glass of Coca-Cola, with four spoonfuls of sugar stirred into it,

> He's a genius all right, but Jesus, how he eats!
>
> *'Tricky Sam' Nanton.*[122]

Ellington was too old to be called up after Pearl Harbour, so his main contribution to the war effort – apart from reaching the top of the new rhythm and blues chart with his sole patriotic record, 'A Slip of the Lip (Can Sink a Ship)' – consisted of a series of weekly hour-long broadcasts titled 'Your Saturday Date with the Duke'. They were made on behalf of the US Treasury Department, and their purpose was selling War Bonds. Ellington read out speeches prepared for him to encourage sales. Over a year, there were nearly fifty hours of performances by the band, which is often in a relaxed, swinging mood, perhaps because the broadcasts are largely from locations in restaurants rather than from studios. One broadcast on April 12, 1945, marks the death of President Franklin D Roosevelt: the air had been given over to solemn classical and military music, but an exception was made for Ellington, who played a programme of spirituals and his own pieces, beginning and ending with 'Moon Mist'. The broadcasts gave Ellington the opportunity to introduce new works and return to old ones, covering the whole range of his repertoire. Two other series of recordings were made during the AFM ban, and they have been issued commercially since, so that we know how well the band sounded during those years. Both were made for transcription services which sold them to radio stations: again the band is relaxed and, as in the case of the Treasury broadcasts, performances are not limited by the three-minute demands of 10-inch 78s.

Inevitably, as the war ended, the band had changed. Some younger men had been drafted into the armed forces, some older men had been tired out by the difficulties of touring in wartime. Among a shifting population of trumpeters, the outstanding soloist was Taft Jordan, a fiery player in the Armstrong mode. He took a vacation in 1947 and never came back. 'I slept almost a whole year,' he said. 'I'd had too much road. For a long time I actually slept two or three times a day, and not cat naps, but for two or three hours.'[125] Ben Webster had left in 1943, Juan Tizol in 1944, Rex Stewart in 1945. One afternoon in July, 1946, the band bus was ready to leave Scragg's Hotel in San Francisco, with only Tricky Sam missing. 'Finally, Lawrence Brown, who had the room next to Tricky's, went to see what was keeping his section-mate. Getting a pass key and entering the room, he saw that Joseph Nanton was dead.'[126]

I'm Beginning to See the Light

As the Second World War ended the popular music business in America was being transformed. The AFM recording ban had brought singers into prominence in the studios because they were usually not members of the union: with support from vocal groups they could continue to make new discs for the labels' publicity machines to promote. Performers who had once been simply part of a big band's personnel turned into stars in their own right, and the bands themselves began to decline as fashion moved away from the fanaticism of the Swing Era. Music based on jazz was no longer the idiom favoured by the mass of listeners and dancers. Instead, white audiences were swept up in a succession of musicals packed with hits, headed by Rodgers and Hammerstein's 'Oklahoma!', which opened on Broadway in 1943 and ran for an astonishing 2,200 performances. Their black contemporaries switched to rhythm and blues by the exuberant small groups led by Louis Jordan and the powerful big band of Buddy Johnson. Meanwhile the committed jazz audience fragmented as young fans discovered and revived the New Orleans style and young musicians broke the rules to create modern jazz, initially called bebop because of its surprising accents. In the war of styles that followed the forces of both sides favoured small, improvising ensembles and despised the drilled disciplines of the big swing bands.

Ellington was better prepared than most bandleaders for the changes, with a high profile from the Carnegie Hall concerts which allowed him to charge big fees for performances, and a solid financial base in successful popular songs. He had broken away from his publisher, Robbins, and set up Tempo Music Inc. to publish his own, Billy Strayhorn's and Mercer Ellington's compositions, among others, putting his sister Ruth in charge of the company. He bought her a house, 333 Riverside Drive, and gave the next-door house, 331, to Mercer.

'When I graduated from Columbia in 1941, he said: *We're going to have a music publishing company and you're going to be the president, Ruthie!* Which was a shock, since I was studying to be a biology teacher.'

Ruth Ellington.[127]

Tempo Music's catalogue included songs with lyrics by Don George, the best known of which are 'I'm Beginning to See the Light' and 'I Ain't Got Nothin' but the Blues'. George, a white New Yorker in his mid-30s, appeared in Ellington's dressing-room one day in October 1943 and offered to collaborate with him. He watched Ellington eat a typical meal of steak, chopped liver, lettuce and tomatoes, orange juice, apple pie and ice cream, starting with the pie and ice cream. George wrote: 'It was the start of a collaboration that lasted over thirty years, not only as songwriters but as buddies. We wrote together, we travelled together, we shared hotel rooms, we shared women and most of all we shared an indestructible affection and understanding.'[128] On a professional level, George found Ellington challenging to work with because his method was unlike that of other composers: instead of writing a melody and the finding chords to fit, Ellington simply wrote the chords.

'Duke was discreet in his affairs. His inner life and feeling were hidden behind a charismatic veil of charm. Publicly he was the most charming, most delightful master of ceremonies. Privately he was a romping, stomping alley cat.'

Don George.[129]

Transatlantic travel resumed after the war, and at the end of 1946 Ellington toured for a month with the legendary Belgian Gypsy guitarist Django

Reinhardt. Recordings of a concert in Chicago show that Reinhardt, using an unfamiliar electric guitar, played alone or with skeletal accompaniments by the rhythm section or the orchestra. The concert saw the premiere of a new Ellington-Strayhorn extended work, 'The Deep South Suite,' of which only one movement was recorded in the studio on the next visit: 'Happy-Go-Lucky Local' is one of Ellington's programmatic pieces about railway trains: this one leaves the station with a

Reinhardt and Ellington on tour in 1946

lot of huffing and puffing from piano and bass, and winds up hurtling down the track with the whistle squealing, as impersonated by Cat Anderson's trumpet.

In 1947 an Ellington musical, with book and lyrics by John Latouche, opened on Broadway: 'Beggar's Holiday' was a variation on 'The Beggar's Opera', using a mixed-race cast headed by Alfred Drake, the star of 'Oklahoma!', with Marie Bryant, who had been one of the 'Jump

William Alonzo 'Cat' Anderson (1916–1981) joined in 1944 as a growl player, but Ellington soon used his phenomenal high notes. His nickname came from his slanting eyes. Musicians became wary of him later because he suffered from a compulsion to steal.

for Joy' singer-dancers. In a landmark year for integration it opened on 5 April, ten days before Jackie Robinson made his debut for the Brooklyn Dodgers, the first African-American in major-league baseball. Robinson played ten years for the Dodgers, but 'Beggar's Holiday' lasted only 108 performances, and before

Ellington could record any of the music the label he had joined in 1946, Musicraft, fell into financial difficulties and had to buy back his contract. Ellington went to Columbia – his adversary John Hammond had left the label – and at his initial session, in Hollywood on 14 August, 1947, recorded one 'Beggar's Holiday' song, 'Women (They'll Get You)', as a comedy vocal for Nance. The date also produced 'H'ya Sue', a bouncy piece introduced by the plunger of Tyree Glenn, sitting in Tricky Sam's chair but with a different, gentler approach, and 'Lady of the Lavender Mist', a dreamy ballad in which the soloists were Hodges, Carney and Brown, plus Jimmy Hamilton, taking the place of Bigard.

Jimmy Hamilton (1917–1994), on the right with Ellington and Ben Webster, had a cool, liquid sound on clarinet, influenced by Benny Goodman. He was an exciting, bluesy soloist on tenor saxophone, but did not care for the instrument.

Hamilton was a well-trained musician and a skilful arranger, contributing scores with a bebop touch to the book. He complained later that Ellington would never perform his scores as written, but always revised them until it suited him. Ellington treated his and Strayhorn's new compositions the same way: at dances he would hand out parts and the band would play the piece, even if it had no ending, the audience unaware that they were listening to unfinished work.[130]

Tom Whaley, the former conductor at the famous Apollo Theatre in Harlem, was hired in 1941 to produce parts for the band members. Whaley explained later: 'Juan Tizol, he did the copying before I come in there, see, and Juan said, No, I ain't going blind copying Duke's music.'[131] Ellington orchestrated his compositions as he wrote them, typically giving each group of instruments a separate stave: one for the trumpets, one for trombones, and so on. He wrote pieces in concert pitch, as if for violins, but most musicians in the band were playing transposing instruments, which sound higher or lower than the written pitch: a trumpeter reading C will sound a tone lower, B flat. So someone had to 'extract' what Ellington had written, writing out each part in the key the instrumentalist expected, then copy out separate parts for each man to read on his music stand. Whaley usually stayed in New York, but Ellington wrote while he travelled, and wanted to hear the music as soon as possible. He might work on a piano in his hotel room, or in a train or a bus, so it was useful to have a skilled extractor and copyist on the road. After Juan Tizol, the work was done by another valve-trombonist, John Sanders, the trumpeter Herbie Jones and the bassist Joe Benjamin.

Toby Hardwick stormed off the stage of the Howard Theatre in Washington and out of music one night in 1946, apparently because of a row with Ellington over a woman. The new lead alto was Russell Procope, who had been with John Kirby's inventive group which billed itself 'The Biggest Little Band in the Land.' Procope also played an earthy clarinet, but was under-used as a soloist. The procession of great bassists continued: Junior Raglin, who had the daunting task of stepping into Blanton's shoes, succeeded admirably, except that he preferred to go on stage in carpet slippers. His successor in 1945 was Oscar Pettiford, a bebop pioneer and one of the all-time masters of the instrument, whose impeccable intonation was matched by his imagination as a soloist. After him came Wendell Marshall, Blanton's cousin, who inherited his rich tone, powerful swing and the bass he had used. Early in 1953, when Marshall was ill, his deputy was Charles Mingus, an innovative virtuoso on the instrument and one of the most influential composers and bandleaders of his generation. He had to leave after four days because of a fight with Tizol.

For five years the tenor saxophone star was Al Sears, a crowd-pleaser in the 'tough tenor' tradition, who recorded memorable solos on 'The Blues' in 'Black, Brown and Beige' and on 'The Suburbanite'. In 1949 he was followed by Charlie Rouse, a Washingtonian with a distinctive sound. On the eve of a European tour Rouse discovered that he had neither a passport nor the birth certificate needed to acquire one. 'There was I standing on the dock waving goodbye to them,' he remembered.[132] Rouse's career developed in the modern jazz field, and he became world famous as a member of Thelonious Monk's quartet between 1959 and 1970. Jimmy Forrest, also hired in 1949, left the following year and had a big hit under his own name with 'Night Train', adapted without credit from 'Happy-Go-Lucky Local'. Then Ellington hired Paul Gonsalves, who was to play a unique role in the re-incarnation of the band.

Ellington's first post-war trip outside North America came in 1948, but the band was left behind when he went to Britain. He had tried to repeat the success of his first visit the following year, 1934, but the British Ministry of Labour, lobbied by the Musicians' Union, withheld work permits, and in 1935 the Ministry 'announced they would no longer grant permits for the Ellington orchestra or any other band to play in Britain until satisfactory reciprocal arrangements had been made with the

American Federation of Musicians'[133] for British musicians to play in the United States. The band passed through Britain in 1939 after touring Scandinavia, but only to catch the boat home: the Ministry of Labour stated baldly: 'We do not allow foreign dance bands or orchestras to give performances in this country'[134]. For the 1948 tour only Ellington, Ray Nance and a singer, Kay Davis, arrived in London, and were allowed to work as variety artists, backed up by a London-based trio led by the bassist Jack Fallon with the guitarist Malcolm Mitchell and the drummer Tony Crombie. After two weeks at the London Palladium they spent another fortnight touring England and Scotland, losing a date at Nottingham's main concert venue: the Rev. Frank T. Copplestone, minister of the Albert Hall Mission, said: 'We felt it seemed hardly the standard of concert we like to have in the hall – which, after all, is our church . . . We aim to let the hall be used for civic and social functions and high-class concerts.' The tour took Ellington to Belgium and Switzerland, ending in Paris.

Mercer Ellington, after studying music at Columbia University, the Institute of Musical Art and Juilliard, had taken out his own first band in 1939, spent two years of wartime service as a trumpeter in a band under Sy Oliver, the great arranger for Jimmie Lunceford and Tommy Dorsey, and gone back to bandleading, without much success or much encouragement from his father. In 1950, though, Duke put him together with the journalist and composer Leonard Feather to run a label called, at Feather's suggestion. Mercer Records. They began to release sessions in the Ellington small-group tradition, mostly under the name of The Coronets, with Strayhorn and occasionally Ellington on piano: the two recorded their party-piece, a duet named after a card game, 'Tonk'. Al Hibbler had a success with 'White Christmas', and 'Perdido', with Pettiford playing cello, became what Feather called 'our solitary near-best-seller.'[135] Pettiford, who was now leading his own band at the modern jazz club, Birdland,

and being promoted on radio, was the label's chief artist. Then 'Pettiford got to drinking Moscow Mules at Birdland and had a terrific argument with the bosses, who fired him,' Mercer wrote. 'That was the end of the airtime.'[136] The company stopped producing records, and Ellington went back to Columbia records. Mercer worked at various times as a salesman and a disc-jockey.

By 1951 even the most successful big bands were in trouble: Count Basie was reduced to leading a small group. For Ellington the blow came when Johnny Hodges announced that he was leaving the Ellington band to form his own group, opening on 9 March at the Blue Note in Chicago, one of Ellington's favourite residencies: a recording session six days earlier produced a hit record, 'Castle Rock', for the impresario Norman Granz, who was backing the band. With him Hodges took Lawrence Brown, Ellington's other star soloist, and Sonny Greer, his oldest musical associate now that Toby Hardwick had left. The loss of Greer might not have been hard for Ellington to bear. For one thing, Greer was drinking heavily and becoming unreliable: for another, his approach to percussion as a source of orchestral colour, although it added to Ellington's palette of timbres and was visually pleasing, was part of an outmoded style. The rhythmic drive of the early Ellington band had come from the leader's left hand and the thrust of Freddie Guy's banjo. When Guy gradually changed to the more fashionable guitar in the early 1930s, the quieter instrument worked alongside Wellman Braud's powerful bass, and that continued into the era of Blanton and his successors, who brought a new flexibility to the double-bass part, putting more of the time-keeping duties on to Guy. Then, in Chicago in 1949, nearly a quarter of a century after joining the Cotton Club band, Guy gave in his notice. To Ellington *Getting rid of the guitar was a useful economy.*[137] But Sonny Greer said he missed Guy's metronomic pulse, and other members of the band knew how much Greer needed support on occasions when he had to drive the band forward in swing style. Rex Stewart, his feud with Williams over, recalled: 'Cootie and I always sat near the drums and, whenever Greer wasn't putting the beat down hard enough, we would both whip his flagging rhythm until it moved and swung . . . I'm sure that anyone who heard us stomping and grunting and exhorting, "Sonny, come on, umph, grab it! Umph! Whip 'em, Nasty, umph," etc. would have thought we were crazy. But it worked.'[138] For a European tour in 1950 Ellington took along an extra drummer, Butch Ballard: 'We had both of our drumkits set up on stage,' Ballard said later. 'He had his full kit on a special riser that was built for him. I was set up down on the stage right between Duke's piano and bassist Wendell Marshall . . . I used a standard four-piece drumkit and played the swing pieces like "A-Train", just straight-ahead jazz. I didn't do press rolls or anything like that. I just kept it swinging right along. Sonny would play on pieces like "Frankie and Johnny" and "Ring 'Dem Bells". Two different styles altogether.'[139] Ballard

Louie Bellson, born in 1924 and christened Luigi Paulino Alfredo Francesco Antonio Balassoni, brought an engaging and enthusiastic personality to the band. *He has the soul of a saint.*[140]

said that after the tour he heard that Ellington and Greer had fallen out, and was offered the drum chair; but he turned it down because Duke wanted him to change his method and use two bass drums.

The bold solution to Ellington's personnel problems became known as 'The Great James Robbery'. The trumpeter Harry James was finding work hard to come by for his band: one of its members was Juan Tizol. He returned to the Ellington fold, bringing with him Willie Smith, a brilliant lead alto and soloist, and Louie Bellson, a innovative drummer who combined power, delicacy and swing. James said: 'If I were them, I'd have done the same thing.'[141] Tizol's importance was in his facility on the valve-trombone, which could execute fast passages along with the saxophones as an important part of Ellington's tonal palette. Smith, for all his fluency, did not have Hodges's breadth of tone or passionate blues phrasing. Bellson, though, brought not only ability but showmanship: he had invented the use of a pair of bass drums and made spectacular use of them in solos that not only pleased the crowds but had genuine musical interest, in an era when the drum solo would become a required item in every jazz concert. Bellson brought along his own arrangements for drum features, 'Skin Deep' and 'The Hawk Talks', the Hawk being Harry James's nickname because of his prominent nose. Bellson left the band after two years so that he could work with his wife, the singer Pearl Bailey, and lead his own groups. But Ellington called him back to the band when there were difficult jobs to be done such as the musical pageant 'My People' and the 'Second Sacred Concert', and hired a series of two-bass-drum players, Dave Black, Sam Woodyard and Rufus Jones.

The newcomers had an immediate effect. 'The most important gain was the spirit these new men brought to the band, and Bellson was a vital factor in this respect,' wrote Eddie Lambert, remarking on the 'enthusiasm and zest which permeates the performances from this period.'[142]

Around the upheaval, a new band was taking shape. Two new trumpets had been hired. One was Willie Cook, a former Dizzy Gillespie sideman, *potentially the best first trumpet player in the business.*[143] Cook, with Gonsalves, Nance and the singer Jimmy Grissom, formed a clique known as the 'air force', because they were so high on drugs. The other new trumpeter was Clark Terry, an individualistic player with a chuckling tone and a humorous imagination, who produced an inventive blues solo on 'Bensonality' in his first recording session on 7 December 1951. At the same session Harold Baker was the trumpet soloist on 'Harlem', or 'A Tone Parallel to Harlem', one of Ellington's most important extended works. It takes the listener on a walk through the neighbourhood on a Sunday morning, using a theme like a spiritual, introduces people in a friendly mood including *a real hip chick. She, too, is in a friendly mood.* In the climactic march *you may hear a parade go by, or a funeral, or you may recognise the passage of those who are making our Civil Rights demands.*[144] 'Harlem' appeared on an LP – the medium had been pioneered by Columbia – with remakes of 'The Mooche', 'Take the "A" Train' and 'Perdido', plus Bellson's drum showcase 'Skin Deep', which was a juke-box hit on two sides of a single. In 1950 Columbia had issued another LP called 'Masterpieces by Ellington', a set of extended arrangements of old pieces and one recent one. But otherwise the label's Ellington output had been aimed at the singles market, and that policy continued in 1953 when Ellington moved to the Hollywood-based Capitol Records. The search for a hit single was at Ellington's insistence, said his Capitol producer, Dave Dexter. The first Capitol recording was 'Satin Doll', made as an instrumental without what Billy Strayhorn's biographer, David Hajdu,

Clark Terry, born in St Louis in 1920, left Ellington in 1959 and became the first black musician on the NBC studio staff, as well as playing in the Gerry Mulligan Concert Jazz Band, leading his own bands and singing comedy numbers like 'Mumbles'.

described as 'oedipal' lyrics, 'an ode to Strayhorn's mother'[145], but those words are lost. The masterly Johnny Mercer, one of Capitol's founders, supplied the familiar ones in 1958, and the composer Alec Wilder wrote: 'It's a soft-spoken, underplayed little song with a marvellous, perfect Mercer lyric, and it truly swings.'[146] It would prove to be Ellington's last hit as a songwriter. The search for record sales led to releases to fit the craze of the day: 'Bunny Hop Mambo', 'Twelfth Street Rag Mambo', a mambo version of 'Isle of Capri'. Side after side featuring Jimmy Grissom, oddest of Duke's succession of dud singers, whose mannered delivery often suggested that someone was trying to strangle him. Among the singles there were two LPs which made an impression on jazz audiences. 'The Duke Plays Ellington', using only the rhythm section, shone an unprecedented spotlight on the leader's piano, never previously heard at such length. 'Ellington '55' showed the band to be in good form. It contained well-known Ellington material, including 'Black and Tan Fantasy' with Nance in Miley's role, and a charging 'Rockin' in Rhythm' with Carney, playing clarinet, taking over from Bigard. There were also tunes associated with other leaders---Count Basie's 'One O'clock Jump' and Lionel Hampton's 'Flying Home', for example---and arranged by outsiders. 'So a degree of mystery attaches to this period in Duke Ellington's career,' wrote Stanley Dance. 'Why, you may ask, did he hire outside arrangers like Gerald Wilson, Buck Clayton and Dick Vance, or assign compositional tasks to Jimmy Hamilton and Rick Henderson, while he and Billy Strayhorn, widely regarded as the best in the business, failed to maintain their normal level of creativity?'[147] Ellington's major extended work of the period, 'Night Creature,' the most impressive of his works using strings, had its premiere at Carnegie Hall on 16 March, 1955, with Ellington and his band performing with Don Gillis conducting the Symphony of the Air, the successor to Toscanini's NBC Symphony Orchestra. But the piece had to wait eight years for a recording. In May, after a session which included 'Discontented Blues', an old number re-titled to make a point, and a valedictory 'So Long', Ellington left Capitol, with no hits since 'Satin Doll' and no new recording contract on offer.

While 'Beggar's Holiday' was in preparation for the stage Ellington had been on the road and left Strayhorn to do much of the work, together with Luther Henderson, a fellow Juilliard pupil of Mercer Ellington and a respected composer and arranger. They decided in 1954 to write a show of their own, called 'Rose-Coloured Glasses', were encouraged to believe they had a potential Broadway hit, and told Ellington they were forming a partnership. Fearing that he would lose Strayhorn, Ellington convinced Henderson that he could make his own way to the top without Strayhorn, and probably told Strayhorn that he did not need Henderson. The Broadway plan petered out. Strayhorn by this time was drinking heavily 'He drank just constantly,' said Marian Logan. 'If he was down, he drank to drown it, and if he was up, he drank to celebrate.'[148] At the end of 1955 he went to Paris to visit Aaron Bridgers, who had been there since 1947 and was working as a cocktail pianist in a gay night club.

In the United States the big nightclubs in city centres were closing down as people who could afford to visit them moved to the suburbs, and the mammoth cinemas were being emptied by television and could no longer support bands to back up movies. Ellington was forced to travel further between jobs and accept more one-night stands, with lay-offs between them. In June he took the band into Eliot Murphy's 'Aquashow', a family variety evening of high divers, ice skaters and comedians played at the Aquacade, part of the huge arena which had been built in the New York suburbs at Flushing Meadow for the 1939 World's Fair. Ellington played a medley of his hits and left another conductor to do the rest of the show. 'He had come upon hard times,' said Mercer. 'He wanted the band to stay together and as a result when the jobs became few he kept the band organised so he didn't care where he had to get the money from, whether it was royalties or whatever.'[149] Business was bad for Johnny Hodges, too. He broke his band up, and on August 1, the day before the 'Aquashow' ended, he rejoined Ellington. Nobody knew it, but the band had turned a corner.

Diminuendo and Crescendo in Blue

Afterwards Ellington would declare: *I was born in 1956 in Newport, Rhode Island.*[150] It was an acknowledgement that one performance of one composition featuring one musician had suddenly resurrected the reputation of the Ellington band as a popular attraction capable of drawing crowds and selling records. The place was the third Newport Jazz Festival, the number was 'Diminuendo and Crescendo in Blue', and the soloist was Paul Gonsalves.

The festival organiser, George Wein, wrote later: 'Duke came to the festival in the middle of a discouraging critical and commercial slump. The band had not been faring well in recent years . . . It was this festival appearance that launched the next highly successful phase of Ellington's career.'[151] Hired to close the festival on the 7th of July, Ellington began the final concert at 8.30 pm with a depleted band, short of two trumpeters and a clarinetist and using a substitute bass player. They played 'The Star-Spangled Banner', 'Black and Tan Fantasy' and 'Tea for Two', a feature for the trumpeter Willie Cook. Then they gave the stage over to a series of unrelated small groups, returning, at full strength, at 11.45 p.m. with 'Take the "A" Train', followed by a newly-written three-part 'Festival Suite', 'Sophisticated Lady' and 'Day In, Day Out', a feature for Jimmy Grissom. Then came numbers 107 and 108 in the Ellington band book, 'Diminuendo in Blue' and 'Crescendo in Blue', written in 1937 and first issued on either side of a 10-inch 78. The original compositions are medium-to-up-tempo blues with no space for improvised solos. The gap originally occupied by turning the record over became, in live performances, filled with an interlude, at first another of Ellington's blues-based pieces such as 'I Got it Bad and That Ain't Good' or 'Transbluency'. Some time in the early 1950s the interlude was handed to Paul Gonsalves to fill with a tenor saxophone solo: a record made at a concert in Pasadena, California, on 30 March, 1953, suggests that he had the audience screaming and whistling at the end of a mere half-dozen choruses. At Newport he played 27 choruses.

'Somewhere around the seventh chorus, it happened,' George Wein recalled. 'A young blonde woman in a stylish black dress sprung up out of her box seat and began to dance. She had caught the spirit, and everyone took notice – Duke included. In a few moments, that exuberant feeling had spread through the crowd. People surged forward, leaving their seats and jitterbugging wildly in the aisles . . . The audience was swelling up like a dangerous high tide'[152] Ellington wrote: *Paul Gonsalves, Jimmy Woode and Sam Woodyard lifted that stone-cold audience up to a fiery, frenzied, screeching, dancing climax.*[153] He brought out his most eminent soloist, Johnny Hodges, for two numbers, and then Ray Nance, to sing and play his feature, 'Tulip or Turnip'. Wein, nervous about 7,000 fans howling for more music, ran on stage and grabbed the microphone in an attempt to end the show. Ellington pleaded to play one more tune, and when Wein refused, to be allowed to

In America's 19th-century Gilded Age the rich built Newport's vast mansions, which they coyly called 'cottages'. There was little to do in summer, one cottage-owner, Elaine Lorillard, remarked in 1953 to George Wein, a pianist who ran a Boston jazz club. Mrs Lorillard's husband, Louis, whose family were tobacco millionaires, helped Wein, against opposition from stuffier Newport grandees, to launch the First American Jazz Festival the following July. An invasion by rock fans interrupted the annual events in 1971: by then the festival had reached non-jazz audiences through the films 'Jazz on a Summer's Day' and 'High Society', with songs by Cole Porter performances by Frank Sinatra, Grace Kelly and Louis Armstrong.

say goodnight. Wein let him have the microphone – and Ellington promptly announced Sam Woodyard's drum solo, 'Skin Deep', starting the crowd yelling again. After that, the band played 'Mood Indigo', and over it Ellington said goodnight and told the fans that he did love them madly. In retrospect, Wein acknowledged Ellington's power over the audience: 'This was a crowd to be reckoned with, appeased. And so Duke Ellington gave them what they wanted. He gave them more than they could ever hope to absorb.[154]'

Paul Gonsalves (1920–1974) was nicknamed 'Mex', although he was born in Boston into a community from the Cape Verde islands off the coast of Senegal. Hired by Ellington because he knew Ben Webster's solos by heart, Gonsalves turned out to be even more under the influence of Don Byas's harmonic experiments. His solos slithered unpredictably between tonalities, but held listeners by their rhythmic drive. Alcohol and heroin made him undisciplined, and he sometimes fell asleep on stage, but Ellington tolerated his lapses and wrote: *His purity of mind suggests to me that he would have made a good priest. His punch line, of course, is 'Jack Daniels', but that is just a kind of façade.*[155]

Gonsalves's solo was less impressive to many who heard it on record rather than at the festival. The Ellington expert Eddie Lambert wrote regretfully: 'The famous – or infamous – Gonsalves interlude follows the pattern he always used on extended solos. He introduces and repeats blues phrases, examining various ways of phrasing them and investigating countless variants. His rhythmic attack is very swinging, but over a solo of such length the lack of sustained development becomes rather trying.'[159] The musician and critic Max Harrison denounced the performance for the 'rape and murder' of a composition he admired.[160] Nevertheless, the LP 'Ellington at

Sam Woodyard (1925–1988) continued the Ellington preference for drummers with a pair of bass drums. He lacked the finesse of his predecessor, Dave Black, but his use of shuffle rhythm and backbeat lent a primitive power to the band. Woodyard said: 'Drums can be very exciting. People used to go to battle to the sound of drums. Drums made them feel like fighting.' Ellington praised him for *No crash bang, never overpoweringly loud, volume just where it should be.*[157]

Jimmy Woode (1928–2005) – pronounced 'Woody' – became the band's bass player in Boston in 1955 on George Wein's recommendation, after Wendell Marshall left to work in the studios. *No matter which way we turned, melodically or harmonically, Jimmy Woode was right on top of it,*[158] wrote Ellington. Woode left the band in 1959 and moved to Europe, based in Sweden, Germany, Holland and Austria and working with the Kenny Clarke-Francy Boland Band and visiting Americans.

Newport', which combined 'live' and studio recordings to re-create the occasion, was the biggest seller of his career, and few Ellington concerts afterwards were complete without what Duke came to describe as a 'wailing interval' for Gonsalves, in 'Diminuendo and Crescendo' or another blues – he played 37 choruses on July 28 at Westport, Connecticut, and claimed to have played 66 choruses in Des Moines, Iowa, when a member of the audience challenged him to go on as long as on the record. The ecstatic reception from the Newport crowd helped to hoist Ellington on to the front cover of the 20th August issue of 'Time' magazine – although the portrait for the cover had been painted in June, so the idea of a story had been suggested before Newport. The article said the concert showed that Ellington 'had emerged from a long period of quiescence and was once more bursting with ideas and inspiration.'[161]. Columbia records, which made the festival recording under a freelance arrangement, now signed Ellington to a longer contract, which would be extended into the 1960s.

In fact the band that created Ellington's renaissance had been completed by the return of Johnny Hodges and the hiring of Woodyard and Woode, who had a remarkable partnership despite their different personalities and approaches to music. After hearing the band in January, 1956, when it was resident at Café Society in New York, Down Beat compared it with Count Basie's and concluded that Ellington 'now has the most under-rated band in the country.'[163] It proved itself in recordings made immediately afterwards. First came 'Blue Rose', a showcase of Ellington and Strayhorn numbers for the singer Rosemary Clooney, in which she and the band achieve such unanimity that it is scarcely credible that the band was recorded in New York and Clooney in Hollywood. Although Columbia were keen to follow her hits for them – songs such as 'Mambo Italiano' and 'Come On-a My House' – Clooney was pregnant with her fourth child and under doctor's orders not to fly. Strayhorn, newly returned from Paris, went to stay with her in Beverly Hills and selected songs that suited her range in between nursing her through bouts of nausea. 'He'd make me crackers and milk,' Clooney remembered. 'I felt a bit better one day and he baked me an apple pie.'[164] Recording a backing track and a singer separately was an innovation: the band recorded Strayhorn's arrangements or re-arrangements of standard material on January 23, mainly sight-reading them. Strayhorn took the tapes back to California to record Clooney. Her clear, unaffected diction and natural swing are perfectly matched by Strayhorn's arrangements, particularly in 'Sophisticated Lady' and 'I'm Checkin' Out, Goom Bye'. Hodges has a powerful feature on Strayhorn's 'Passion Flower', announcing his return. But the album fell between the jazz and pop audiences, and sales were disappointing.

Not surprisingly things began to look up in 1956. By this time Pop had realised that he had to play more piano to hold everything together.

Mercer Ellington.[162]

Rosemary Clooney: a long-distance collaboration

The second album was made in February for the independent label Bethlehem, under the title of 'Historically Speaking', and therefore consists chiefly of earlier pieces in new recordings, the bulk of them from the 1940s. One was 'Ko-ko', in the first commercial recording since the 1940 original, and lovers of Ellington's music were almost universally shocked and distressed by it. Most prominent was the composer and critic André Hodeir, who accused Ellington in the Paris magazine, 'Arts', of making 'a hideous copy of his own masterpiece.'[165] The 1956 'Ko-ko' was taken much faster than the original's menacing medium tempo: Eddie Lambert pointed out that Ellington had speeded up performances immediately after the 1940 recording, but none of them has the dismissive quality of the 'Historically Speaking' version, which sounds as though Ellington and the band can't wait to finish it. 'Ko-ko' has sometimes blinded listeners to the rest of the album: in the revived numbers and two new ones – Ellington's 'Lonesome Lullaby' and Strayhorn's 'Upper Manhattan Medical Group' – the band demonstrates unity and relaxed swing, with richness of blend in all sections, particularly the saxophones. A session in Chicago in March, kept in the 'stockpile' which Ellington now began to build up, and not released until after his death, shows the solo strength, with strong contributions from Clark Terry on 'Uncontrived' and 'Short Sheet Cluster'. Terry's companions in the trumpet section were Willie Cook, Cat Anderson and Ray Nance, who also played the violin. The trombones were Britt Woodman, Quentin 'Butter' Jackson, the plunger specialist, and John Sanders on valve-trombone. The alto saxophones were Hodges and Russell Procope, the tenors Gonsalves and Jimmy Hamilton, who took most of the clarinet solos. Harry Carney played baritone as usual, and Ellington, Woode and Woodyard were the rhythm section. With only one long-term change in personnel---when Harold Baker rejoined the trumpets in 1957, eventually replacing Cook – this was the band

Ellington was to lead for the next three years into a new era of recordings tailored to the growing market for LPs. As a basis, it had a new agreement between Ellington and Strayhorn, forged over dinner at the Hickory House nightclub in Manhattan soon after Newport. Strayhorn told friends that Ellington had seen big possibilities, for which he would need Strayhorn's help, that *From now on, your name is up there, right next to mine.* And the first undertaking, said Strayhorn, would be 'a Shakespeare thing.'[166]

It had to wait, though, for a project which Ellington had already sold to Columbia. It was an allegorical history of jazz called 'A Drum is a Woman', describing the love affairs of the mysterious Madame Zajj, who begins life as a drum. The plot takes her from Africa by way of the Caribbean, New Orleans and New York to the moon, and at each stop she meets a man, each named Joe. The story, based on sketches begun in Hollywood during the 'Jump for Joy' period, became not only a record but a television special, narrated by Ellington and danced by the leading African-American dancers Carmen de Lavallade and Talley Beatty. In the New Orleans section, Ellington asked Clark Terry to impersonate Buddy Bolden, born, in the words of the narration, *with a silver trumpet in his mouth*, a near-legendary jazz pioneer who left no surviving records. Terry protested that nobody knew anything about Bolden, and Ellington answered: *Oh sure. Buddy Bolden was suave, he was debonair, and he was just a marvellous person, he had beautiful ladies around him, had a big sound, he tuned up in New Orleans and across the river in Algiers he would break glasses he was so powerful. He loved diminishes. You know all these things.* He says: *You ARE Buddy Bolden! Play me some diminishes and bent notes!* So I started playing and he said, *That's it! That's it!* Terry added: 'He could masterfully psych you into doing exactly what he wanted you to do.' [167] Critics were not kind, finding the humour misplaced: even for those days some of the lyrics were ill-judged:

It isn't civilised to beat women
No matter what they do or say
But will somebody tell me
What else can you do with a drum?

But Ellington himself, when the journalist Derek Jewell asked him in 1966 which of his pieces had given him the most satisfaction; answered: *Of the big things, 'A Drum is a Woman', and some of my early songs. They're not big pop successes, you know, but in all of them you feel the weight of joy.*[168]

Duke Ellington, Billy Strayhorn, 1965 – London

Ellington and Strayhorn had worked more closely than ever before on 'A Drum is a Woman'. Strayhorn told an interviewer: 'We just kind of did everything. He wrote lyrics, I wrote lyrics. He wrote music, and I wrote music. He arranged, and I arranged.'[169] The 'Shakespeare thing' began on a similar level of collaboration.

Just after Newport the Ellington band had played at the music festival associated with the annual Shakespeare Festival at Stratford, Ontario: they were expected to bring a major new work, but played a conventional set of Ellington pieces, heralded by 'Hark, the Duke's trumpets!', a re-titling, from 'King Lear', of a composition also known as 'Bass-ment', 'Daddy's Blues', 'Discontented Blues' and 'Trombone Trio'. The festival's musical director, Louis Applebaum, said Ellington 'realised he had missed an opportunity and offered to come back next year with something special. Also, while he was here he became very, very close to our director of musical promotion, Barbara Reed, and there was no question whatsoever that their closeness had a great, great deal to do with Ellington's sudden enthusiasm for Stratford.'[170] Strayhorn, a devotee who had 'Shakespeare' as one of his band nicknames, prepared by re-reading his copy of the complete works. Dissatisfied with Ellington's proposed title, 'The Shakespearean Suite', he considered 'Nova' – Avon spelled backwards. Townsend, hunting through Bartlett's 'Familiar Quotations', found 'Such Sweet Thunder', a phrase from 'A Midsummer Night's Dream' describing a bear-hunt, which had the advantage of incorporating a pun on 'suite'.

As completed, the work consists of twelve short movements, dedicated to one or more of Shakespeare's characters or plays. It makes a satisfying and cogent whole, apart from the finale, 'Circle of Fourths', another excursion on the blues for Paul Gonsalves. Otherwise the solo stars are called up to take such roles as Henry V (Britt Woodman), Julius Caesar (Jimmy Hamilton), Jimmy Woode (Othello). In Strayhorn's 'Up and Down, Up and Down' three pairs of instrumentalists depict the lovers in 'A Midsummer Night's Dream,' while Terry plays their tormentor, Puck, ending the piece by using his trumpet to speak the phrase: 'Lord, what fools these mortals be!' Ellington's 'Madness in Great Ones' is about Hamlet, a piece of conflicting rhythms underneath Cat

Anderson's high-note trumpet. In fulfilment of Ellington's promise, the album cover says the suite was 'composed and orchestrated by Duke Ellington and Billy Strayhorn', but it was mainly Ellington's work. Having advanced the deadline from the Stratford festival in July 1957 to a concert at the Town Hall auditorium in New York in April, Ellington encouraged Strayhorn to re-use two pieces he had written the previous year, both of them re-titled to feature Johnny Hodges in evocations of Romeo and Juliet, and of Cleopatra on the Nile. Apart from 'Up and Down', wrote the Dutch Strayhorn scholar Walter van de Leur, 'other than scoring a small section for Ellington's opener of "Such Sweet Thunder", Strayhorn apparently had little to do with the other nine movements . . . the larger part is genuine Ellington, and ranks among his best writing.'[171]

The public premiere of 'Such Sweet Thunder' and the broadcast of 'A Drum is a Woman' were followed by a tour of one-nighters: one of them was recorded, at the Sunset Ballroom in Carrolltown, Pennsylvania, a farming community with a population two-thirds the capacity of the 1,500-seat Town Hall. The orchestra that produced such disciplined performances for studio records of the new pieces plays its familiar repertoire for dancers in a relaxed but alert way, showing that its members could enjoy sharing a night out with an appreciative audience. They were soon back in the studio to make a Duke Ellington Song Book with Ella Fitzgerald, the third in a series which producer Norman Granz had begun with Cole Porter and continued with Rodgers and Hart. It had been planned for a long time, and was intended to use about four dozen songs from the Ellington-Strayhorn repertoire. Fitzgerald had already recorded fifteen of them with a small group led by her regular pianist of the time, Paul Smith, and the ex-Ellington tenor star, Ben Webster. When she and the Ellington band had assembled at the studio for a four-day session, Strayhorn had brought thirteen arrangements. Ellington had brought one. 'It was a panic scene with Duke almost making up arrangements as we went along,' Fitzgerald said later. 'Doing it that way, even if it was fun at times, was kind of nerve-racking.'[172] The tension drove Fitzgerald to tears at one point, and she seldom sounds comfortable. A hasty adaptation of 'Rockin' in Rhythm' pits her against the full strength of the Ellington trumpet section, five men at the time, plus Dizzy Gillespie sitting in; Strayhorn's new arrangement of 'Take the "A" Train' carries her near to the bottom of her range, where she sounds colourless. On the other hand, for 'Day Dream' Strayhorn bathes her in mysterious dark tones, making the most successful performance of the date. Ellington filled the

Mahalia Jackson (1911–1972) was the leading singer of African-American gospel music, and a commercial success with hits such as 'Didn't it Rain'. Born in New Orleans and orphaned at the age of four, she went to live in Chicago as a teenager. She learned to sing from the records of Bessie Smith ad Louis Armstrong. But as a born-again Christian she refused to sing blues or jazz, believing them to be sinful

gaps with a four-part 'Portrait of Ella Fitzgerald', constructed on the spot out of scribbles on the back of envelopes, and recorded with fulsome spoken introductions, on a day when Fitzgerald was not in the studio and therefore not embarrassed by being treated as the heroine of a fairy-tale. Another set of songs was left for her to record with another Webster group: both small-band sessions give her the relaxed settings to help her to do the songs justice.

Ellington spent two years planning to the project to re-record 'Black, Brown and Beige', according to Irving Townsend's original sleeve note, and throughout that time intended to include in it the great gospel singer Mahalia Jackson, who was under contract to Columbia. The result is very different from the 1943 version recorded at Carnegie Hall, and less ambitious even than the extracts made in the studio for Victor. For Columbia in February 1958 Ellington used only the first part, 'Black', and concentrated on its second movement, 'Come Sunday'. With Hodges temporarily in Florida, working with a Strayhorn group, Ellington split his solos between Carney and Baker. John Sanders, who took over Tizol's introductory solo, was to leave the band the following year to study for the Roman Catholic priesthood. Jackson's role came in an additional performance of 'Come Sunday', with lyrics added. Then she sang the 23rd Psalm, with an orchestral background. The following day, when she reappeared in the studio, Ellington asked her to sing 'Come Sunday' unaccompanied, with the lights out, and that recording has now been issued with the rest of the original LP. Clearly the presence of Jackson and the absence of 'Brown' and 'Beige' alter the piece from being 'A Tone Parallel to the History of the American Negro' into being a predominantly devotional work. *This encounter with Mahalia Jackson had a strong influence on me and my sacred music*, Ellington wrote.[173]

By now Ellington and Townsend were launched on a series of what were later called 'concept albums', including 'Ellington Indigos', a collection of ballads, mostly not Ellington's own, and

'At the Bal Masque', apparently inspired by masks decorating the nightclub of a Miami Beach hotel. Ellington and Strayhorn arranged a bizarre selection of songs including 'Who's Afraid of the Big Bad Wolf?' and 'The Donkey Serenade'. Critics hated it, but Eddie Lambert wrote: 'Ellington will always be remembered as a man of real humour, and this aspect of his personality is given full rein.'[174] The unifying factor in 'The Cosmic Scene' was its use for an entire LP of a small group, billed as Duke Ellington's Spacemen – the trombones, the rhythm, and three of the more modern solists, Hamilton, Gonsalves and Terry. Hamilton contributed several arrangements, balancing the solo group against trombone backgrounds. Terry has a brilliant solo on 'Spacemen' and more opportunities than Ellington usually gave him in nightly performances, at which he and 'Perdido' were inseparable. 'Newport 1958' brought together new pieces performed at that year's festival, though the album, once again, was a mixture of location and studio recordings with applause dubbed in. As a surprise it included 'Happy Reunion', a feature for Gonsalves that is, for once, not a work-out on the blues but a ballad, beautifully played with the rhythm section. And soon afterwards, the American festival season over and the boost from Newport still fresh in the minds of fans, the Ellington orchestra was on its way to Europe.

The Single Petal of a Rose

In Britain for the first time since 1933, the Duke Ellington orchestra, arrived at Plymouth on board the French liner 'Ile de France' on 3 October, 1958. Two days later, on a rainy nigh in London, the band was on stage at the Royal Festival Hall for two concerts with a total attendance of 6,800, and British audiences saw the pattern of Ellington's presentations: the band, when enough members had assembled, being stomped off into 'Take the "A" Train' by Harry Carney's foot, and Duke himself delaying his entry until the crowd was warmed up. 'A big, portly man, tapering down to ballet-type pumps, with a pouchy, laconic face,' Kenneth Allsop wrote, and expressed the puzzlement so many fans felt that the show included such oddities as Ray Nance's comedy dancing and 'Autumn Leaves' sung in French by Ozzie Bailey, 'which had a touch of the Winter Garden tea rooms.' In his dressing room afterwards, Ellington explained: *All the audience weren't jazz addicts. We cater for all tastes.*[175]

Broadcasters obviously influence public taste, and Ellington's ASCAP record for the year beginning 1 October 1958 to 30 September 1959 shows that on American radio and TV stations the Ellington title most often heard was 'Caravan', with 440 playings, followed by 'I'm Beginning to See the Light' with 272 and 'Don't Get Around Much Any More' with 244. His most recent hit, 'Satin Doll', was played 111 times, 'Diminuendo in Blue' nine times and 'Crescendo in Blue' five.

The British tour took Ellington to Leeds for an international arts festival at which he gave four performances for a flat fee of

£4,500. At a reception on 18 October he was introduced to Queen Elizabeth II, who had not been to his concerts. *I told her she was so inspiring and that something musical would come out of it. She said she would be listening, so I wrote an album for her,* Ellington told the writer Neil Shand later. *Only one record has been issued and that is with the Queen . . . It was written for her and there is no point in dedicating something to the Queen of England and then just publicly releasing it.*[176] To the frustration of fans outside the royal family, it was not until 1976 that 'The Queen's Suite' was issued commercially from the 'stockpile': it proved to be one of Ellington's most attractive works, brilliantly played by the band. One movement did become part of his repertoire: it was 'The Single Petal of a Rose', a serene Debussy-like piano solo. It seems to have had its first performance near the end of the British tour at a party given by some London friends, Leslie and Reneé Diamond, at their flat off Park Lane. 'Observing that one petal had fallen from the bunch of roses on the piano, Duke produced the beautiful melody of "Single Petal" for the enraptured guests.'[177]

The Musicians' Union and the American Federation of Musicians allowed the Ellington band into Britain under new rules which let US players work in Britain in exchange for British musicians touring in the United States. Louis Armstrong, Count Basie and Stan Kenton were among the earlier imports: Ellington visited in exchange for the band led by trombonist Ted Heath.

After a two-month European tour the band returned to the United States and another attempt to make a hit out of 'Jump for Joy', this time in a Miami Beach nightclub, where the show was booked to run at least a month. It opened on 20 January, 1959, but closed on 6 February. Ellington took the band back to New York and into the recording studios. A new album, 'Ellington Jazz Party', pretended to be just that, with applause dubbed on. Some of the record came from a session with nine extra percussionists tackling two pieces Ellington had played to a 10,000-strong audience at Lewisohn Stadium, then part of the City College of New York, the previous summer. 'Tymperturbably Blue' used a row of tympani, and 'Malletoba Spank' called for two vibraphones, two xylophones, glockenspiel and marimba – all the new colours were made part of the Ellington sound-world. Another session brought in the former Count Basie singer Jimmy Rushing for a rousing blues, and Dizzy Gillespie took a brilliant trumpet solo on 'U.M.M.G.', named after Dr Arthur Logan's Upper Manhattan Medical Group. Rushing was under contract to Columbia, like Ellington, but Gillespie was under contract to Verve, owned by Norman Granz, who had just managed Ellington's European tour. In exchange Ellington had to play on two sessions for records led by Johnny Hodges, another Granz artist. The records, 'Back to Back' and 'Side by Side', show Ellington the informal pianist, unconcerned about anything except his own solos and accompaniments in small-group jazz. Almost all the tunes are blues, and the format is that of a jam session, with the drummer Jo Jones to propel it. Their success heralded a series of collaborations between Ellington and guest musicians.

But first there was a movie to make. In early May Ellington went to stay in northern Michigan, the home ground of a lawyer, John D Voelker, who wrote novels under the name Robert Traver. Otto Preminger was to produce and direct 'Anatomy of a Murder', shooting on location in the area, and Ellington would not only provide the score but play a part. The role, naturally enough, is of a piano-player, Pie Eye, who leads a group in a country roadhouse where a small-town attorney and amateur pianist, played by James Stewart, likes to hang out. In his one scene, Duke shares a keyboard with Stewart, who thanks him for letting him sit in: the screenwriter, Wendell Mayes, perhaps a little over-anxious to be hip, makes Duke reply: *Hey, you're not splittin' the scene, man? Ha? I mean, you're not cuttin' out?* Ellington's music, recorded in

Hollywood at the end of May, helped to give the picture style, as did the titles by Saul Bass, but the score's most effective part is probably the stratospheric coda by Cat Anderson which accompanies the end titles. In fact, there is no underscore for most of the picture's later part, which takes place in a courtroom and has Stewart surrounded by three hungry young Method actors – Lee Remick, Ben Gazzara and George C Scott – and a real judge playing the part of a judge. Preminger considered Ellington for two later movies, but by that time the fashion was over for jazz scores – it had started with Miles Davis's improvised music for Louis Malle's thriller 'Ascenseur pour l'échafaud' in 1957 and reached a peak with Johnny Mandel's score for Robert Wise's 'I Want to Live' in 1958.

Ellington's next film had jazz as its subject, so a jazz score was appropriate. 'Paris Blues' told the story of two American expatriate musicians, Paul Newman and Sidney Poitier, who meet two women tourists, Joanne Woodward and Diahann Carroll. 'That both romances were mixed-race matches was an element of the film that contributed significantly to Ellington's agreement to take on the project.'[178] But the distributors insisted on a re-write to segregate the couples into black and white. Ellington and Strayhorn moved to Paris to work on the film, which also had Louis Armstrong in a cameo role as a trumpeter, Wild Man Moore: Strayhorn's former lover, Aaron Bridgers, got a part as pianist. The score includes new versions of Ellington and Strayhorn standards as well as specially-composed pieces: it is more closely integrated with the picture than 'Anatomy of a Murder'. Two numbers showcase Armstrong with a mixture of American and French studio musicians in Paris: 'Wild Man Blues' is a scrappy evocation of a jam session, and 'Battle Royal' is an anonymous-sounding flag-waver.

But Ellington and Armstrong soon afterwards went into a New York studio together, in April 1961, and left a lasting legacy in sessions for which Ellington took the piano chair with Armstrong's regular band, the All-Stars. They played 16 Ellington standards and one song, 'Azalea', which Duke had written 20 years earlier with, he claimed, Louis in mind. None of the tunes was central to the restricted repertoire Armstrong used in his later years, but he is supremely confident, sometimes apparently more at home with the material than his clarinet-player of the time, the distinguished old Ellingtonian, Barney Bigard. Ellington himself – as we can hear on rehearsal tapes discovered and issued by Michael Cuscuna, an expert in the reconstruction of recording sessions – takes charge gently within the small-band swing context Louis favoured, and sets moderate tempos and dynamics which show off Armstrong's gleaming sound.

The following year Ellington recorded with another jazz pioneer, Coleman Hawkins, the father of the jazz tenor saxophone, in a session reminiscent of one of the Ellington small groups of the 1930s, using material of that period such as 'Wanderlust' and 'The Jeep is Jumpin'' with new pieces in a similar style including a 'Self-Portrait' for Hawkins, a bouncing 'You Dirty Dog' and a couple of Latin-rhythm tunes. On one of them, 'Limbo Jazz', Woodyard chants along with a simple riff, unaware that the tape is rolling. Hawkins was enjoying an Indian summer of his talent, and his turbulent phrasing in solos contrasts with the more urbane Johnny Hodges and the other Ellingtonians, while his big sound gives an extra punch to the ensembles.

A month later came a quartet recording for the same producer, Bob Thiele of Impulse! Records, with another tenor giant, John Coltrane, at that time the hero of the avant-garde, and formerly a sideman in Johnny Hodges's band. It starts with a lyrical 'In a Sentimental Mood', but afterwards Coltrane seems to go into his shell, and Ellington himself sounds more adventurous than the young lion. The recording engineer, Rudy van Gelder, recalled: 'John was really awed in Duke's presence.'[179] The week before,

Ellington had joined two masters of the generation before Coltrane's for a trio session: the drummer was Max Roach, one of the founders of bebop, and the bassist was Charles Mingus, whose few days in the Ellington band had ended after his fight with Juan Tizol. During a session watched by many critics, Mingus became upset and took his bass out of the studio: Ellington had to persuade him to return.

Last in these encounters with outsiders was the most ambitious: the Ellington band in the same studio and playing at the same time as the Count Basie band. Basie was contracted to Roulette records, producers of the Ellington-Armstrong album: in exchange Roulette had to lend Basie to Columbia, Ellington's label. Since the mid-1950s Basie had led a band which purred or roared like a well-drilled pride of lions depending on the music in front of it: its members were as disciplined and positive as the Ellington men were unpredictable and temperamental. Its arrangements came from a variety of composers and arrangers, some within its ranks: its leader edited them and unerringly chose tempos. It had a powerful character of its own, soloists of the first class, and a well-known repertoire. For the meeting at Columbia's big studio on 30th Street, the tunes were shared out, an equal number from each book, and the bands sat alongside each other so that Basie's would be heard on the left channel of the stereo mix and Ellington's on the right. The unanimity and sheer weight of sound are, at least on recent CD transfers, impressive and exciting, and several tracks contain duets in which the two leaders demonstrate their very different approaches to the same basic style of piano.

The Ellington band's recording work on its own concentrated on re-creations. The album 'Piano in the Background' revived

'We were supposed to be the hot young guys, but we were scrambling. Duke had that left-hand stride thing going, his real sharp sense of time.'

Max Roach[180]

Basie and Ellington

standard pieces such as 'Rockin' in Rhythm' and 'Main Stem',
but with prominent solos by the piano-player – the 'background'
was where he would ordinarily have been. The same sessions, on
the West Coast, produced 'Nutcracker Suite', a witty set of
re-orchestrations of Tchaikovsky in which Ellington and Strayhorn
also found new titles, so that 'Waltz of the Flowers' became
'Dance of the Floreadores' (and, incidentally, ceased to be a waltz)
and the 'Dance of the Sugar-Plum Fairy' turned into 'Sugar Rum
Cherry'. The lightly-textured arrangements trip through the
dances, giving particular opportunities for solos to Jimmy
Hamilton's clarinet, its acid tone coming into its own. Some
critics sneered, accusing Ellington and Strayhorn of disrespect.
Before they could have read the attacks, they were back in the
studio within days to record five extracts from Grieg's incidental
music to 'Peer Gynt'. Most of these they treated, respectfully, as
tone poems newly voiced to fit the Ellington palette: the results
are often stodgy. For the Monterey Festival in 1960 Ellington and
Strayhorn wrote 'Suite Thursday', a punning title based on a novel

set in the town, John Steinbeck's sequel to 'Cannery Row'. *The critics at the festival didn't dig the suite too well, but when the record eventually appeared there were a lot of reversed opinions. It wasn't the first time we had experienced that sort of thing!* [181] Not long afterwards came 'Piano in the Foreground', a trio album showing what Ellington could do with three ballads by other composers, one forgotten song from 1936 and seven new pieces of his own, when he had the support of his own rhythm section: Woodyard on drums and another great bassist, the rich-toned Aaron Bell, who had replaced Jimmy Woode. The band's brass section had also changed: Clark Terry had left the trumpets, Butter Jackson and John Sanders had left the trombones. Ray Nance had become the band's primary trumpet soloist. The great reed section hung together. In the spring of 1960 there was a surprise: Lawrence Brown came back to the trombones, to stay for nine years. And 1963 saw the return of Cootie Williams, most powerful of the growl trumpets.

While the 'Nutcracker Suite' sessions were going on, the band was booked to appear at Gene Norman's club on Sunset Strip in Los Angeles, alongside the comedian Mort Sahl. Both Ellington and Sahl had contracts which said they should be top of the bill, and when Ellington saw that he was billed below Sahl he failed to appear, leaving the band to play without him and claiming to be ill, although he went on working at the record studio. The leading African-American newspaper, the 'Chicago Defender', quoted a report by the Associated Negro Press saying that the club was 'conforming to the popular practice on stage and on television of top-billing white entertainers over Negroes, even when the talents and greater reputation of the latter are evident'.[182] After five days Norman cancelled the band: one of his staff pointed out that Sahl was part-way through a 20-week engagement and Ellington was booked for only two weeks.

During a residency at the Riviera Hotel in Las Vegas in January 1961 the drug squad raided the apartment Ray Nance was sharing with other members of the 'air force': Paul Gonsalves, and the trumpeters Willie Cook and Fats Ford. Ellington bailed them out of jail, but Gonsalves and Nance later faced prosecution for narcotics possession. Gonsalves got probation, but Nance had to serve two months in prison because he had a previous drug conviction. For some years the band was blacklisted in Las Vegas.

Tourist Point of View

During an earlier residency at the Riviera in Las Vegas, in the spring of 1960, Duke Ellington met the woman who would be his frequent companion for the rest of his life. Fernanda de Castro Monte saw Ellington on stage and came to the Riviera every night, so that she got fired from her job as a singer at the Tropicana, one of the other hotel-casinos on The Strip. She became, she said, Ellington's slave. She monopolized his time between shows, and when the long Riviera engagement ended and the band got on the train for Los Angeles and the 'Nutcracker Suite' sessions, she was at the station to see Ellington off. Mercer said: 'She was very smartly dressed in a mink coat. Just as the train was about to pull out, she opened the coat. She had nothing at all on under it, and she wrapped it around him to give him his good-bye kiss. With that, she left him to cool off.'[183] Known as the Countess or Contessa. Fernanda was twenty years younger than Ellington and, according to Don George, 'a tall, strikingly handsome blond lady who stood bold, with her boots and her suede pants and suede suits with slits at the sides. She could be forceful or humble.'[184] She helped to improve his diet: 'Steak, ham and eggs, English jams were what he really enjoyed – mixed with oddities like lettuce sprinkled with sugar – but for Fernanda he would at first eat or drink almost anything,' wrote Derek Jewell.[185] Ellington picked up her taste for caviar and vodka. According to Mercer, Fernanda was 'the fifth and last lady in his life with whom he was *deeply* involved – my mother, an actress, a dancer, a showgirl, and a chanteuse.'[186] She traveled with Ellington to Mexico and to the

East and on many European trips. The writer Jeremy Hornsby, anxious to talk to Ellington for the London 'Daily Express' in 1963, caught up with the band at rehearsal in Copenhagen, then traveled in the band bus on the ferry to Sweden, where they were staying, back to Copenhagen for the performance, and finally on the last ferry back to Sweden and Ellington's hotel suite. But Duke refused to be interviewed until the Countess's two poodles had been fed, and hotel staff were dispatched to grocers' shops in Helsingborg in search of their usual diet: Rice Krispies. The interview began at 3 am with the dogs munching in the background.[187] The Countess missed some trips, as when Ellington brought the band to Britain in 1969. Larry Westland, now executive director of the educational charity Music for Youth, was hired to travel with him and stayed in hotel rooms adjoining Ellington's. Away from the Countess's influence Ellington indulged himself. 'We used to call room service and get them to send up every crème caramel they had,' said Westland. 'At the Piccadilly in Manchester they sent about fourteen and we ate them all.'[188] At the Dorchester in Park Lane Westland discovered that Ellington had gone to bed with a woman who turned out to be an American student.

In 1962, after Frank Sinatra launched his own record label, Reprise, Ellington left Columbia Records to join him, with autonomy to produce his own albums and other jazz records. The first sessions where other bandleaders'

'Despite the fact that he was involved with so many women, I would say that, apart from his mother and sister, he had a basic contempt for women. He spent so much time celebrating and charming them, but basically he hated them.'

Mercer Ellington.[189]

'I think Edward regarded women as flowers, each one lovely in their own way, and they absolutely adored him, it was shocking! I couldn't believe it, absolutely shocking! The way women fell on their faces in front of him, you know?'

Ruth Ellington.[190]

Duke Ellington in 1962 by Chuck Stewart

theme songs under the title 'Will the Big Bands Ever Come Back?', and later Ellington would record 'A Spoonful of Sugar', 'Hello, Dolly', 'Moon River' and 'I Want to Hold Your Hand'. His own compositions were on the superb 'Afro-Bossa' and on 'The Symphonic Ellington', recorded around Europe with local orchestras' string sections playing alongside the Ellington band. The performance of 'Harlem' starts with Cootie Williams pronouncing the word Harlem, at first quietly and then at full power: it still has the spine-tingling effect it had when Ellington and Cootie performed it in the Royal Albert Hall on 19 February 1967 with the London Philharmonic Orchestra under John Pritchard. The recorded performance, though, lacks the unity of others by the band without strings, and the most interesting piece on the record is 'Night Creature', a ballet which begins with a movement about, as Ellington put it, *a blind bug who comes out every night to find that because he is the king of the night creatures, he must dance*.[191] About the same time, in Paris, Ellington recorded a small-group session with a three-man string section: Ray Nance, the French violinist Stephane Grappelli and the Dane Svend Asmussen, playing the viola. Despite the very different styles of the three fiddlers, the result is unmistakably Ellingtonian. Another session starred the Swedish singer Alice Babs, who worked with Asmussen in a band called the Swe-Danes and was to have an important role in Ellington's late work. With Paris-based musicians except for Strayhorn and Ellington himself, she performed for this recording mainly in the wordless tradition begun by Adelaide Hall, but with her own wide range, rich tone and uncanny intonation. Later Sinatra and Ellington agreed to collaborate on an album called 'Francis A and Edward K': to give opportunities to the band's soloists the LP would consist of long versions of only eight songs. Only one of them, 'I Love the Sunrise' from 'The Liberian Suite', would be by Ellington. Perhaps fearing Ellington's lack of preparedness, Sinatra got the brilliant arranger Billy May to do the writing, and May brought the charts to Ellington well in advance. A disastrous rehearsal made it obvious that the Ellington men, great improvisers though they might be, were not the sort of slick sight-readers who dominate studio work. Ellington promised to play the arrangements every night for a fortnight during his shows, filling in Sinatra's vocal part on the piano, so that his men could learn them in the same way they learned his own music. On 11 December, 1967, with Sinatra ready to start the recording session, May gave a downbeat and realized 'they never touched the charts again; they never even looked at 'em after that day.'[192] May brought in studio players to lead the sections and save the album: he concluded that the Ellington men 'had started to go to pot although they still had that distinctive sound.'

Ellington went to Chicago in August 1963 to help commemorate the centenary of the Emancipation Proclamation. For the 18 days of an exhibition marking a Century of Negro Progress, he brought a pageant called 'My People'. The music used adaptations from 'Black, Brown and Beige', and the twice-daily performances employed some of the band, four singers, and a tap-dancer, Bunny Briggs, to perform a new version of 'Come Sunday' under the title 'David Danced Before the Lord.' Like Alice Babs's singing, Briggs's dancing became an element in the Sacred Concerts which Ellington would begin two years later.

Although Ellington insisted that it was not a political work, 'My People' included a number called 'King Fit the Battle of Alabam'', which celebrated the peaceful mass protests led by Martin Luther King, Jr., against segregated facilities, beginning with sit-ins at Birmingham lunchrooms and culminating when President John Kennedy ordered troops to end Governor

'Working with Duke is an inspiration. You have to create, and sometimes I feel as if I'm dancing on a cloud.'

Bunny Briggs.[193]

George C. Wallace's refusal to allow black students into the University of Alabama. King, who spent eleven days in jail during the campaign, attended a rehearsal and met Ellington: the two men embraced. 'My People' was still running when King led a march of 250,000 civil rights protestors on Washington on 28 August and made the 'I have a dream' speech about equality and freedom.

On tour in Britain on 20 February 1964, Ellington taped a concert for 'Jazz 625', a series for the new BBC-2 television channel, transmitting on the improved 625-line standard. The channel was due to start broadcasting on 20 April but was stopped by a power black-out: the Ellington show went out the next night at 11.00 pm. At the start of the tour, on 15 February at the Royal Festival Hall, the 29-year-old British saxophone star Tubby Hayes 'went to the concert in the hope of getting a spare seat before going to his own club job and found himself drafted into the empty chair of the absent sax player, Paul Gonsalves.'[194] Hayes later called it 'the most memorable experience of my life.'

The U. S. State Department had discovered that jazz could be a weapon in the Cold War, a way of influencing the hears and minds of people in Asia, Africa and Latin America as the weakened European powers loosened their grip. Louis Armstrong and Dizzy Gillespie had taken part in State Department-sponsored tours: early in September 1964 the Ellington band went to the Middle East and the Indian sub-continent, beginning in Damascus. The tour, scheduled to last 14 weeks, produced the inspiration for what would be one of Ellington and Strayhorn's most imaginative later suites, and the band members traveled comfortably in good hotels and without having to fend for themselves when they needed to eat. But at the second stop on the tour, Amman, Jordan, Ray Nance was either taken ill or offended VIPs or caused a problem with his drug use. He was sent back to the U.S. and the leader of the band at the Ambassadors Hotel, New

Delhi, found himself filling the Ellington band's fourth trumpet chair until a substitute could be flown from America. In New Delhi, too, Ellington himself fell ill and the band had to travel on without him for a few days. Arthur Logan went to him: 'I found him there physically in pretty good shape but pretty badly depressed. Edward said he had never seen such poverty.'[195] In Ankara, the capital of Turkey, on 22 November, the tour was abruptly cut short: President Kennedy had been assassinated. 'Edward was beside being beside himself,' said Marian Logan. 'He had a big problem with death – not just his own, but anybody's. He couldn't deal with it.'[196]

The following year Mercer Ellington became the bands's road manager, taking the place of the long-serving Al Celley, whose eyesight was failing. The fourth trumpet chair also went to Mercer, a forlorn-looking figure who sat at the end of the row and never took a solo. The brass section's soloists were much reduced: in the trumpets were Cootie Williams and Cat Anderson, filling his specialized role in the stratosphere, though a piece recorded as 'Jungle Kitty' and 'Miaow' gave him a chance to half-valve like Rex Stewart; in the trombones Lawrence Brown took virtually every solo, learning to use the plunger. Sam Woodyard, unreliable through drug use, was eventually replaced by the heavy-handed Rufus 'Speedy' Jones, and elegant John Lamb became the bassist after Ernie Shepard fell ill. Still the reeds held together. This was the band that recorded 'The Far East Suite', an eight-part journey based on scenes the farthest east of which is the Indian 'Bluebird of Delhi'. The LP on which it first appeared included a separate, more easterly, piece, the Japanese-inspired 'Ad Lib on Nippon', the

'Guys like Paul Gonsalves, Sam Woodyard and Ray Nance were really in other worlds. When they played for Duke, those disparate worlds came together. Duke knew just how to use their artistry.'

George Wein.[197]

Duke and Mercer Ellington, with bassist Joe Benjamin

result of a 1964 visit: Jimmy Hamilton claimed that he wrote it, although it is credited to Ellington. The suite begins with 'Tourist Point of View', with a sinuous Gonsalves solo over complex rhythms, a response to the East 'fresh to the inexperienced eye of the West – exotic, dramatic and strange, a world "upside down",'[198] and includes 'Isfahan', a tribute to the former capital of Persia and a showcase for Johnny Hodges's luxurious alto. Exotic influences were to inspire many of Ellington's later compositions, such as 'The Latin-American suite', 'The Goutelas Suite' and 'The Afro-Eurasian Eclipse'.

In 1965 the three members of the music jury for the annual Pulitzer Prizes, deciding that no composition submitted to them was worthy of a prize, put forward Ellington's name for a special award to recognize his forty years of work. The fourteen-member board which administered the prizes for New York's Columbia University turned down the plan and two jurors resigned in protest, throwing the normally-secret proceedings of the Pulitzer selection into the public arena.

Fate is being kind to me. Fate doesn't want me to be famous too young.

Ellington covered his wounded feelings with a typically urbane joke about fate, but resented being pigeon-holed by musical snobs. *The word 'jazz' has been part of the problem. It never lost its association with those New Orleans bordellos. In the nineteen-twenties, I used to try to convince Fletcher Henderson that we ought to call what we were doing 'Negro music'. But it's too late for that now.*[199]

In September he went to San Francisco to take his place in a year of celebrations for the consecration of the Episcopalian (or Anglican) Grace Cathedral, which had been more than half a century in building. Ellington presented what proved to be the first of three 'Sacred Concerts', his most controversial works since 'Black, Brown and Beige' – some of which he incorporated. 'A Concert of Sacred Music' is just what it is: an assemblage or patchwork of earlier pieces in new versions, such as 'New World A-Comin'', the miniature piano concerto from 1943, and 'Come Sunday', under that title and in the tap-dance version, 'David Danced Before the Lord', from 'My People'. The loose structure meant that the running-order could be changed at Ellington's inspiration or to cope with circumstances: at San Francisco, for instance, the numbers using a group of singers were brought forward because a delayed start was putting them at risk of missing their flight back to southern California and their day jobs. Louie Bellson, brought back to the band for the occasion, provided a masterly drum solo, but the music throughout was subservient to the message, some of which is crudely stated, as in the strange idea of having the choir chant the names of the books of the Bible in sequence. Some of this embarrassed listeners, and disagreements carried on through the second and third concerts in 1968 and 1973, though Derek Jewell also pointed out that the concerts were 'disarmingly direct and simple – perhaps too much so for some sophisticated tastes.'[200] Ellington himself told the congregation in San Francisco: *I'm certain this is the most important statement we have ever made.* He gave the concert about fifty times, in between engagements in dance halls, theatres and nightclubs.

The East Coast premiere was on 26 December at the 5th Avenue Presbyterian Church in lower Manhattan, and the running order was altered again to insert a Christmas song: Billy Strayhorn played the piano and his close friend, Lena Horne, sat next to him on the piano bench to sing it. It was nearly two years since Arthur Logan had found Strayhorn exhausted outside the Logan apartment and sent him for tests: the diagnosis was cancer of the oesophagus, a disease associated with heavy drinking and smoking. He had radiation therapy and operations, eventually being obliged to take liquid food directly into his stomach. Dr Logan had him cared for at the Hospital for Joint Diseases, then located in East Harlem: Logan's wife Marian visited him there often, and so did Strayhorn's lover, a white graphic designer named Bill Grove. Ellington telephoned every day, but did not visit: 'Edward couldn't see him like that,' said Marian Logan. 'He couldn't take that.'[201] Strayhorn sent a new feature for Johnny Hodges, and the band performed it from his manuscript: later it got the title 'Blood Count'. It was his last piece. In the early morning of 31 May, 1967, Billy Strayhorn died at the age of 51: Bill Grove was with him. Lena Horne was in Europe, Marian Logan was in Canada, and Ellington was working at a casino in Reno, Nevada, when Dr Logan phoned to tell him. Marian Logan said: 'Arthur said: 'Are you going to be all right?' And Edward said, *Fuck no, I'm not going to be all right! Nothing is all right now.* And Edward just cried.'[202] Later he sat alone in his hotel room and wrote about Strayhorn. At a memorial service on 5 June, at St. Peter's Evangelical Lutheran Church at Lexington Avenue and 54th Street in Manhattan, Ellington read out his tribute to *Poor little Swee' Pea*, ending with the words:

His patience was incomparable and unlimited. He had no aspirations to enter any kind of competition, yet the legacy he leaves, his oeuvre, will never be less than the ultimate on the highest plateau of culture (whether by comparison or not).

God bless Billy Strayhorn.[203]

Praise God and Dance

By the end of the 1960s, Duke Ellington's performances, at least so far as European audiences were concerned, began to follow a familiar routine. The members of the band would saunter, one by one or in small groups, on to the stage before an impatient audience which was often puzzled by the identities of unfamiliar faces. Harry Carney was still pounding his foot to set the tempo for 'Take the "A" Train', and the theme was still a fanfare for the piano-player waiting in the wings. Ellington retained his elegance and his preference for blue clothes, often giving the impression of a man who had been taking his ease in a favourite smoking-jacket with a good cigar and a cognac. The look of relaxation was enhanced by the lightweight pumps he had specially made and always wore on stage: it was given a hint of night-club sleaziness by the way he had chosen to wear his hair long at the back so that it spilled over his collar. Along with the medley and the Gonsalves marathon there was a version of 'Satin Doll' as a background to a monologue in which Ellington taught the audience how to be cool: *Tilt the left ear-lobe* on *the beat and snap the fingers on the* after-*beat . . . and so, by routining one's finger-snapping and choreographing one's ear-lobe tilting, one discovers that one* can *be as cool as one wishes to be,* all leading up to a reminder that *We* do *love you madly.*[204] Ralph Ellison, a former trumpeter and author of the great African-American novel 'Invisible Man', wrote: 'He is one of the most handsome of men, and to many his stage manners are so suave and so gracious as to appear a put-on – which quite often they are . . . However, Ellington's is a creative mockery in that it

Duke Ellington at the White City TV centre London, in 1965

rises above itself to offer us something better, more creative and hopeful, than we've attained by seeking other standards.'[205]

On record his first project after Strayhorn's death was an album in tribute to his collaborator, '. . . And His Mother Called Him Bill', consisting of Strayhorn compositions. The band plays in its most polished manner, and there are solos from former members: Clark Terry on 'Boo-Dah' and 'U.M.M.G.', and, taking Tizol's valve-trombone solo on 'Rain Check', John Sanders, on his way to becoming a monsignor. Even Cat Anderson is kept away from the top register and given plunger solos instead, on 'Charpoy' and 'All Day Long'. But the emotional core of the record is its final track: as the band-members pack instruments and talk among themselves at the end of a session, we hear Ellington at the piano quietly beginning to play 'Lotus Blossom'. Gradually the conversation is silenced. Afterwards Ellington said: *That was what he most liked to hear me play.*[206] Ellington began to end some concerts with the tune.

The following January, Ellington brought his 'Second Sacred Concert' to the vast spaces of the Cathedral of St. John The Divine, an unfinished Episcopalian leviathan on Manhattan's Amsterdam Avenue at 112th Street. Although the lyrics are once again naive at best, much of the musical material this time was new, and this has been generally regarded as the most successful of Ellington's church works. He used dancers – including Geoffrey Holder, husband of Carmen de Lavellade, from 'A Drum is a Woman' – three choirs, rehearsed by Tom Whaley, the copyist, and five solo singers, of whom the most important was the Swedish soprano Alice Babs, who took

Alice Babs, born Alice Nilsson at Kalmar, Sweden, in 1924, began singing in clubs at 15. *She sings opera, she sings lieder, she sings what we call jazz and blues, she sings like an instrument, she even yodels,* wrote Ellington. *In referring to her, one never says, 'There are just a few left,' because she was probably the only one born.*[207]

part in the concert and a recording which followed after Ellington asked her to come specially to the United States. Her warmth of tone, sense of swing and ebullient personality – still fizzing with energy as she entered her 80s – shone through in 'Heaven', a wordless song called 'T.G.T.T. (Too Good to Title)' and the finale, 'Praise God and Dance'. Ellington insisted that the concerts were *not the traditional mass jazzed up,* and that *I think of myself as a messenger boy, one who tries to bring messages to people, not people who have never heard of God, but those who were more or less raised with the guidance of the Church.*[208]

In summer 1968 Jimmy Hamilton decided that he was tired of the road, and left the band, ending the great reed section. His replacement was Harold Ashby, a tenor saxophonist in the Webster mould as well as a clarinetist. The tours continued, taking the band for the first time to South America and Mexico.

I regard this concert as the most important thing I have ever done.[209]

But Ellington's vigorous sex life was catching up with him. 'It was no longer a matter of hitting a town, having a fling, and moving on,' wrote Mercer, now able, as band manager, to observe his father at close quarters. 'Women began to cling to him more and more. The world was shrinking because of air travel, and he never knew when and where some of these ladies would show up.'[210] Ellington developed a habit of kissing everybody in a room four times, so that nobody could tell if one or more of the women was his lover. In emergency, he could flee from an over-attentive woman by going home and letting Evie Ellis deal ferociously with telephone calls. Evie had resigned herself to the conclusion that he would never marry her, although she had a moment of hope when his estranged wife, Edna, died in 1966: the same day she told Renée Diamond over the phone to London: 'I'm hoping he'll keep his promise to marry me one day. My guess, though, is that he won't.'[211] Evie knew about Ellington's long-term affair with

Fernanda de Castro Monte, and once burst into the Logans' apartment with a pistol, searching for Ellington, who was hiding in a spare room. Evie also flew to Japan and confronted Ellington while Fernanda was travelling with him: he firmly sent Evie back to New York. Increasingly, she stayed in her apartment and her chief companion was Davy, a little black poodle given to her by the agent, Joe Glaser. 'There was often hardly anyplace to sit in the big living room because of Davy's beds, blankets, food-bowls, and rubber toys,' wrote Mercer.[212]

Ellington with President Richard Nixon at the White House celebration

Neither Evie nor Fernanda was on Ellington's guest list on his 70th birthday, 29 April, 1969, when he went to the White House to be given the Medal of Freedom, the highest honour America can bestow on a civilian. Ellington escorted his sister, Ruth, and other guests included most of the Ellington family, as well as the

Logans, the Diamonds and the Dances. From the band came Harry Carney and Tom Whaley, and from competing bands Cab Calloway, Dizzy Gillespie and Benny Goodman. Mahalia Jackson was a guest, too.

Richard M. Nixon, newly installed as 37th President and five years away from his disgrace and resignation over his abuse of power in the Watergate scandal, had been persuaded to give Ellington the medal by Leonard Garment, a former professional musician who was one of his aides, and Willis Conover, presenter of a regular jazz broadcast on Voice of America, the government propaganda station. Conover was famous for his sonorous bass voice and portentous delivery among jazz fans throughout the world except the United States, where Voice of America is forbidden to broadcast. Ellington, standing with Nixon in the receiving line, surprised him by greeting everyone with his usual four kisses. 'When Nixon inquired why, he gave the reply he had been giving for many years: *One for each cheek,* which Nixon took some time to fathom. Later, at the medal presentation, he saluted the president the same way.'[214] The presentation came after dinner in the State Dining Room, where Ellington's father had occasionally worked. Replying to the

By the 1960s expansion had changed Washington from the city Ellington left as a young man: John F Kennedy summed it up: 'Washington perfectly combines southern efficiency with northern charm.'[213] The year before Ellington's award the district where he had lived as a child was devastated by riots which followed the assassination of Martin Luther King, Jr. on 4 April 1968 in Memphis, Tennessee, at the age of 39. The downtown stores went unscathed, but the black shopping area around 14th and U Street, NW, was ruined by arson and looting. The Howard Theatre closed permanently. After a generation of decline the opening of a Metro station helped to make the 19th-century houses near U Street a target for gentrification in the 2000s.

President's speech, Ellington said: *There is no place I would rather be tonight except in my mother's arms.*[215]Later Nixon himself went to the piano to play 'Happy Birthday' and start the evening's music by an all-star band, later broadcast to the world – except, of course, the USA. After Nixon and his wife, Pat, went to their private apartments a jam session started in the East Room and Ellington led the dancing with Carmen de Lavallade. He got back to his hotel about 3 am, and that evening he was more than a thousand miles away, playing in Oklahoma City.

When it toured Europe late in 1969, the band took on a strange appearance: only two trombones were present and a new recruit to the reeds, Norris Turney, sat with them, playing trombone parts on an alto saxophone – Lawrence Brown, apparently still seething over Ellington's affair with Fredi Washington, retired at the end of the year. A Hammond B-3 organ was on stage, played by 'Wild' Bill Davis, in private a rather shy, reticent man. He had been one of the pioneers of jazz on the instrument and was also a skilled arranger, responsible for the Count Basie version of 'April in Paris' with the famous 'one more time' ending, which Ellington took over. A frequent sideman on recordings made under Johnny Hodges's leadership, Davis was to act for the next two years as a second keyboard-player as well as contributing arrangements to the Ellington book.

The organ was, disturbingly, almost the first sound heard on Ellington's next album, 'New Orleans Suite', establishing the mood for 'Blues for New Orleans', a dramatic setting for one of Hodges's most eloquent solos. Davis does not play on the rest of the album, but the next number, 'Bourbon Street Jingling Johnnies', introduces another new instrument, Norris Turney's flute, and Russell Procope, emerging from Hamilton's shadow, plays a major role on clarinet in 'Second Line', a reference to a street parade. The suite was the result of a commission from George Wein, who organised a festival in the city, and five movements of this major new work were played at the festival and recorded on 27 April, 1970, in New York. Ellington worked to complete the album with four new 'Portraits', of New Orleans musicians: Louis Armstrong, Mahalia Jackson, his former bassist Wellman Braud and the soprano saxophone giant Sidney Bechet. He hoped that as a tribute to Bechet, his mentor, Hodges would play the soprano: he had put the instrument aside in the 1940s because Ellington refused to pay him extra for doubling on it. But Hodges died suddenly of a heart attack in his dentists's waiting room on 11 May. Hodges had been Ellington's most important soloist and one of the few who had been able, for a limited time, to lead bands of their own. Ellington showed a deference to him by programming his solos in the more important second halves of concerts, and part of his act was to hold a page of score for Hodges to apparently read from. But Hodges was not easily mollified for the losses he believed he had suffered because ideas of his had been turned into successful songs published under Ellington's name: when one of them was played he would mime counting money. Rex Stewart wrote: 'Johnny had a strange way of airing his grievances. He was very visible in his front-row saxophone chair near the piano, from where he directed remarks and questions to Ellington, out of the side of his mouth. It was hard for Duke to ignore him, but he always put on that wide, phoney smile and did his best.'[216] Told of his death, Ellington wrote: *Never the world's most highly animated showman or greatest stage personality, but a tone so beautiful it sometimes brought tears to the eyes – this was Johnny Hodges. This is Johnny Hodges. Because of this great loss, our band will never sound the same.*[217] At the recording session two days later, Armstrong was impersonated by Cootie Williams, Braud by Joe Benjamin, a brilliant bassist who had been working for Tempo Music, and Bechet by Paul Gonsalves, on tenor saxophone.

New compositions began to emphasize the solo work of the recruits. A suite, 'The Afro-Eurasian Eclipse', began with a feature for Ashby's tenor on an up-tempo 'Chinoiserie'. The 'Togo Brava Suite', a response to the West African republic's decision to put Ellington's portrait on a stamp in a set including Bach., Beethoven and Debussy, gave Turney's flute an important voice. Turney wrote and played alto on a tribute to Johnny Hodges, 'Checkered Hat'.

Both Ashby and Turney were given distinctive roles, along with Joe Benjamin, in the era after the death of Hodges. Other new musicians were there principally to make sure that the band did not sound scrawny: some, like the trombonist Malcolm Taylor, were inadequate soloists; others were neglected, among them Johnny Coles, an individualistic trumpeter who had made his mark with such demanding leaders as Gil Evans, Charles Mingus and Herbie Hancock. Coles was mainly restricted to solos on 'How High the Moon' and 'Goof', a recent composition on which Ellington himself originally played the solo. In the view of Eddie Lambert, 'Ellington once said that you needed to know how a musician played poker before you could write for him: by the time Coles came in Ellington had neither the time nor the inclination to play poker with his sidemen.'[218] Lambert also pointed out that after the death of the gentle Strayhorn, Ellington seemed, surprisingly, to revert to his jungle days, taking inspiration from exotic places, so that 'there is a resurgence of violent, menacing, "primitive" music of a kind which would have seemed out of character for the smooth sophisticated Ellington of the forties and fifties.' Much of this music went unissued on record at the time: although 'Togo

Norris Turney (1921–2001), born in Wilmington, Ohio, toured with Billy Eckstine and Ray Charles before joining Ellington, and with the revived Savoy Sultans after leaving.

Harold Ashby (1926–2003) worked in Chicago blues bands before moving to New York. He was a friend of Ben Webster, who brought him into the Ellington circle.

Brava Suite' and parts of 'The Afro-Eurasian Eclipse' were performed in public, the studio recordings Ellington made of them became part of the stockpile. Some time in the 1960s Ellington developed the habit of giving each new piece a four-letter code before it got a definitive name. Some of the codes foreshadow the titles: in 'The Afro-Eurasian Eclipse', the piece coded 'Schn' became 'Chinoiserie' and 'Didj' became 'Didjeridoo'; but 'Mich', written around 1967, became 'Acht O'clock Rock', and 'Gong', 'Tang' and 'True' were not re-titled. The codes became known to the public only after Ellington's death, when Mercer Ellington began licensing some of the stockpile for issue. Part of the cost of being his own record-producer was that between September 1970 and June 1971 he ran up a $13,487.93 bill for studio services.[219]

For some years, Ellington had been under contract to write his autobiography, on the basis that Stanley Dance would collaborate with him, and started in the late 1960s to jot down notes. According to the book Mercer later wrote, also in collaboration with Dance, 'The manuscript that eventually materialised was undoubtedly unique. It was written on hotel stationery, table napkins, and menus from all over the world. Stanley became so familiar with the handwriting that he could often decipher it when Pop could not.'[220] On 27 September 1971, while the band was touring in what was then the Soviet Union, Dance gave Arthur Logan a letter to pass on to Ellington, telling him that the manuscript was on its way to the publisher. 'I feel that I've pretty well completed my end,' wrote Dance, 'and I have a hunch you may prefer to work on the titling and routining on your own.'[221] The book, 'Music is My Mistress', appeared in autumn 1973, after a last-minute hitch because the publisher had chosen a jacket in brown, the colour Ellington associated with the death of his mother: he insisted it be changed to blue, and 25,000 brown jackets appeared after his death on a cheap edition. 'Music is My Mistress' is an extension of the Ellington stage character:

charming, witty, ironic and evasive, treating his whole life as a fairytale. It makes no mention of his wife or of any of the women who shared his existence. Mercer said: 'He talks about everybody except himself, it's an old trick of his!'[222] But the book does include a dignified statement of the faith that was by now central to his work.

In January 1973 Ellington had been forced to spend eight days in hospital in Los Angeles with influenza. Later he and other members of the band were examined in Houston, Texas, after Cootie Williams had to stop working because of a chest infection: Ellington and Harry Carney were advised to consult their own doctors when they got back to New York. Arthur Logan sent Ellington to specialists, who diagnosed lung cancer. 'We were told that the disease was advancing rapidly, but he didn't believe it,' Mercer said. 'His absolute faith in God made him believe that he could go on and on, and he did.'[223] Flying overnight from New York, Ellington and the band, with Mercer and, unusually, Ruth Ellington, reached London on the morning of 23 October, 1973,

Ellington and Alice Babs rehearse the Third Sacred Concert in the Abbey

to rehearse for a new 'Sacred Concert', to be performed the following day in Westminister Abbey. Alice Babs flew in from Sweden and Roscoe Gill, by that time a regular collaborator in the sacred concerts, had been in London for a week to rehearse the professional choir. On the day of the performance, United Nations Day, there were more rehearsals: they started badly, when Ellington protested at the presence of press photographers, and lasted long into the evening. Russell Procope, who joined some British musicians and fans in a pub near the Abbey, looked exhausted and was reluctant to return to the platform. Paul Gonsalves had been taken to hospital that morning, too ill from drink or drugs to play. Ellington found the platform almost empty of experienced soloists: Norris Turney had walked off the stand and out of the band earlier in the year because Ellington insisted on increasing the tempo of one of his numbers, making it impossible to play.

When the 'Third Sacred Concert' eventually began, in the confused acoustic of the Gothic abbey, the weight of the solo work fell on Alice Babs, Harry Carney and the composer himself, relieved by Harold Ashby taking over Paul Gonsalves's up-tempo role, and a passage played by Art Baron, a trombonist, on his

I have never been so unprepared to do a performance as I am in this case. [224]

second instrument, the recorder. In the audience, we realized that there were serious difficulties because of pauses in the performance. Derek Jewell wrote: 'Duke was really ill at this time, so much so that he disappeared from the platform for ten minutes in a state of near collapse, leaving Alice Babs and the band to carry on without him.' [225] After the concert the Prime Minister, Edward Heath, gave a party at 10 Downing Street, but Ellington was so weak that he spent only fifteen minutes there. It was Babs who gave the 'Third Sacred Concert' its emotional power: the following night she was on stage with the band in Malmö, Sweden, mainly singing wordless vocals, as Ellington went on with a tour which would take him to Africa and the presentation of an Ethiopian honour by the Emperor, Haile Selassie, before he returned to London and a Royal Command Performance at the Palladium on 26 November. He was hoping that Arthur Logan would be there.

Mercer had sent Logan a first-class return ticket to check on Ellington's health, but his plans changed as the days passed: he told Ruth over the phone: 'I've got this bug – and a lot of things are bugging me.'[226] On 25 November, Logan fell to his death from the elevated Henry Hudson Parkway at 134th Street. Fearing that Ellington might cancel the Palladium show, Mercer and Ruth kept the news from him, and Ellington did the performance and was presented to the Queen as planned. He was not told of his friend's death until 29 November, the day of the funeral. 'For the next two or three days he unashamedly went through moments of mental hysteria,' Mercer recalled. 'He just couldn't cope with the idea that Arthur was gone.'[227] Ellington phoned Marian Logan and said: *I don't know what I'm going to do. I'll never ever get over this. I won't last six months.*[228] Mystery surrounded Logan's death, near a hospital which has been re-named the Arthur C. Logan Memorial Hospital. His widow said he was pushed off the bridge by two muggers: Mercer believed he committed suicide because he was involved with loan sharks.

The tour went on until a last concert, at Finsbury Park in North London, in the former Astoria cinema, a 3,000-seat 1930s picture palace which had become an ill-kempt rock venue

'If he ever lost a friend, it was Arthur. I saw him affected by Billy, but nothing like with Arthur.'

Mercer Ellington.[229]

as the Rainbow Theatre, and is now a church. Ellington spent a long time offstage, handing over a large part of the concert to another piano-player, the Frenchman Raymond Fol. Returning to New York, a reduced band filled the small stand at the Rainbow Grill in the Rockefeller Centre, but Ellington had to go to hospital for several days. Back on the road, he played dates with the band sporadically until 22 March, at Sturgis, Michigan: then, accompanied by Jim Lowe, his valet and road manger, he flew from Detroit to New York, spent a few days resting at home, and moved into the Harkness Pavilion at Columbia Presbyterian Hospital, on Fort Washington Avenue near 168th Street. He had an electric piano brought in, and carried on working obsessively on an opera,'Queenie Pie', in the hope of success on Broadway. He talked to Mercer about a ballet, 'Three Black Kings' and how the tapes of the 'Third Sacred Concert' should be edited for release. Suddenly Evie, too, was found to have cancer, and, after an operation, had to stay at home on West End Avenue. They spoke on the phone. Fernanda de Castro Monte came to visit. On 29 April, his birthday, a concert of some of his sacred pieces was given at the Central Presbyterian Church in New York. On May 15, on a visit to London, Paul Gonsalves died. Three days later Tyree Glenn died, too. Nobody told Ellington, who had pneumonia. Jim Lowe spent the nights in Ellington's room so that Ruth and Mercer could get some rest before sitting with him during the days and evenings. In the early hours of Friday, 24 May, Lowe heard Ellington's breathing stop and called a nurse: at 3.10 am, Ellington was dead.[230]

His body was taken to an undertaker on Third Avenue: for a while it lay there with those of Gonsalves and Glenn. Over the weekend 65,000 people queued to pass by it. Masonic ceremonies were performed: few people had known that Ellington was a Freemason. For the funeral on 27 May, there were 10,000 people in the Cathedral of St John the Divine and 2,500 listening to loudspeakers outside. Stanley Dance gave the address, and Ella Fitzgerald sang 'Solitude' and 'Just a Closer Walk with Thee'. Harry Carney was one of the pallbearers: he died six months later, on 8 October. Ellington was buried at Woodlawn Cemetery, in the Bronx, next to his parents. Evie was too ill to go to the funeral. After a long illness she died on 7 April, 1976, at the age of 64, and was buried next to Ellington. After his death, Fernanda de Castro Monte left New York and went to Europe. In London, on June 12, there was a memorial service at St Martin-in-the-Fields: Humphry Lyttelton played in the band, led by John Dankworth, whose wife, Cleo Laine, sang. Adelaide Hall sang 'Creole Love Call', the song she recorded in 1927.

The day after the funeral Mercer became the leader of the band, and took it to Bermuda for a two-week engagement, without Carney or Russell Procope. He toured with the band and in 1981 took it into the Lunt-Fontanne Theatre on West 46th Street for 'Sophisticated Ladies', a revue based on Ellington music which ran 767 performances, the

Mercer is 'really a better musician than his father'

Edna Ellington.[229]

Broadway hit for which Ellington had striven so long. Mercer completed 'Queenie Pie', a story of war between Harlem beauty parlours, and conducted it in Philadelphia and for a month in Washington. Sonny Greer, who turned out to have been kept on the payroll since leaving the band, went to work with Russell Procope in a trio led by the pianist Brooks Kerr at Gregory's, on First Avenue and 63rd Street, grinning and nodding behind the drums and greeting each customer who came in to hear an all-Ellington repertoire.

Mercer, who had moved his base to Denmark and married a Dane, died of a heart attack in Copenhagen on 8 February, 1996, at the age of 76. His son, Paul, took over the leadership of the Duke Ellington Orchestra. Ruth Ellington went on managing the Ellington business: she was in charge of Tempo Music until she sold the controlling interest to another publisher in 1995. Her first marriage, to a writer, Daniel James, broke up, leaving her

Duke Ellington. 1974

with two sons, Michael and Stephen James. Later she married an operatic baritone, McHenry Boatwright, who died in 1994. Ruth died on 6 March, 2004, after a long illness.

In 1988 the Ellington archive of letters, notes, photographs, scrapbooks and accounts was acquired from the family by the National Museum of American History, part of the Smithsonian Institution in Washington, DC. In New York, the stretch of 106th Street running west to Riverside Drive, where Ellington bought adjacent homes for Ruth and Mercer, was renamed Duke Ellington Boulevard. And in 1999, a hundred years after his birth and twenty-five after his death, the Pulitzer Prize committee finally gave Ellington a special award in recognition of his genius.

Notes

Frequently-cited sources are abbreviated in these notes as follows:
DE, *Music*: Duke Ellington, *Music is My Mistress*, New York, 1974.
ME, *In Person*: Mercer Ellington with Stanley Dance, *Duke Ellington in Person*, London, 1978.
Jewell, *Duke*: Derek Jewell, *Duke: A Portrait of Duke Elllington*, New York, 1977.
Nicholson, *Portrait*: Stuart Nicholson, *A Portrait of Duke Ellington: Reminiscing in Tempo*, London, 1991.
Stewart, *Boy*: Rex Stewart, ed. Claire P Gordon, *Boy Meets Horn*, Oxford, 1991.
Tucker, *Reader*: Mark Tucker (ed), *The Duke Ellington Reader*, New York, 1993.
DEC: Material in the Duke Ellington Collection, Archives Center, National Museum of American History, Smithsonian Institution, Washington, DC.

1. DE, *Music,* p. 6.
2. DE, *Music,* p. 12.
3. Booker T Washington, *Up from Slavery,* (1901) p. 62, Airmont edition, 1967.
4. Neal R Peirce and Jerry Hagstrom, *The Book of America*, New York and London, 1983, p 144.
5. Gore Vidal, *Armageddon?: Essays 1983-87,* London 1987, p. 5.
6. DE, *Music,* p. 6.
7. DE, *Music,* p. 15.
8. DE, *Music,* p. 20.
9. Barry Ulanov, *Duke Ellington,* London, 1947, p. 6.
10. DE, *Music,* p. 23.
11. Nicolson, *Portrait* p. 10, quoting Carter Harman interview collection 1964 #8, DEC.
12. DE, *Music,* p. 9.
13. DE, *Music,* p. 20.
14. as above.
15. as above, p. 21.
16. Nicholson, *Portrait,* p. 168.
17. DE, *Music,* p. 12.
18. Barry Ulanov, *Duke Ellington,* London, 1947, p. 14.
19. Duke Ellington, Foreword to Willie 'The Lion' Smith with George Hoefer, *Music on My Mind,* London, 1966, p. ix.
20. Garvin Bushell as told to Mark Tucker, *Jazz from the Beginning,* Ann Arbor, 1988, p. 77-78.
21. Marc Thompson, *A Visit with Mrs Duke Ellington,* Ebony, March 1959, pp. 132-8.
22. Stewart, *Boy,* p. 33.
23. as above, p. 175.
24. Garvin Bushell as told to Mark Tucker, *Jazz from the Beginning,* Ann Arbor, 1988, p. 34.
25. Dick Wellstood, liner note for *Donald Lambert, Harlem Stride Classics,* Pumpkin 104, Miami, 1977.
26. Constance McLaughlin Green, *The Secret City: A History of Race Relations in the Nation's Capital,* Princeton, 1967 p. 208.

27. Arthur Miller, *Timebends,* London, 1987, p. 46.

28. DE, *Music,* p. 36.

29. As above.

30. Duke Ellington, Foreword to Willie 'The Lion' Smith with George Hoefer, *Music on My Mind,* London 1966, p. x.

31. Willie 'The Lion' Smith with George Hoefer, *Music on My Mind,* London 1966, pp 149-150.

32. As above, p. 151.

33. As above, p. 156.

34. Konrad Bercovici, *The Black Blocks of Manhattan,* Harper's magazine, Oct 1924, quoted in Jervos Anderson, *Harlem, the Great Black Way,* London 1982, p. 172.

35. New York Clipper, 23 November 1923, p. 12, quoted in Mark Tucker, *Ellington: The Early Years,* Oxford, 1991, p. 99.

36. Interview with Inez M Cavanaugh in 'Metronome', November 1944, p. 17, quoted in Tucker, *Reader,* p 464.

37. Nat Shapiro and Nat Hentoff, eds. *Hear Me Talkin' to Ya,* New York, 1955, p. 231.

38. Clarence Major, *Juba to Jive: a Dictionary of African-American Slang,* New York, 1994, p. 217.

39. Stanley Dance, *The World of Duke Ellington,* London 1971, p. 7.

40. Interview with the author, 2 February 2005.

41. Rex Stewart, *Jazz Masters of the Thirties,* New York, 1972, pp. 103-106.

42. Interview by Jack Cullen for radio station CKNW, Vancouver, 30 October 1962, collected in Tucker, *Reader,* p. 339.

43. DE, *Music,* p. 77.

44. ME, *Person*, p. 44.

45. Lena Horne as told to Helen Arstein, *In Person: Lena Horne,* New York, 1950.

46. *Variety,* 7 Decemebr 1927: collected in Tucker, *Reader,* p. 32.

47. Marshall and Jean Stearns, *Jazz Dance,* New York, 1968, p. 236.

48. as above, p. 235: from conversation at Hyannis, Mass., 1966.

49. Stanley Walker, *The Night Club Era*, New York, 1933, pp. 105-6.

50. ME, *Person,* p. 26.

51. Arthur Pollack, Brooklyn *Eagle*, 21 June 1929, quoted in Marshall and Jean Stearns, *Jazz Dance,* New York, 1968, p 154.

52. Constant Lambert, *Music Ho!* London 1934 (Penguin edition 1948, p. 155).

53. DE, *Music*, p. 98.

54. Marc Thompson, *A Visit with Mrs Duke Ellington,* Ebony, March 1959, pp. 132-8.

55. ME, *Person*, p. 48.

56. As above.

57. Gunnar Askland, *Interpretations in Jazz: A Conference with Duke Ellington:* in *Etude,* March, 1947, collected in Tucker: *Reader,* p. 256.

58. Mel Watkins, *On the Real Side: laughing, lying and signifying, the underground culture of Afro-American humor,* New York, 1994, p. 276.

59. Interview with Helen Dance, New York City, May 1976, Smithsonian Jazz Oral History Project, Institute of Jazz Studies, Rutgers, pp. 87-89.

60. Interview with author, 2 February, 2005.

61. Stanley Dance, *The World of Duke Ellington,* London 1970, p. 80.

62. Gunther Schuller, *Ellington in the Pantheon,* in *Musings,* New York , 1986, p. 49.

63. John S Wilson, *New York Times,* May 24, 1974, quoted in John Edward Hasse, *Beyond Category,*

the *Life and Genius of Duke Ellington,* New York, 1993, p 314.

64. Gama Gilbert, *Philadelphia Record,* 17 May 1935, collected in Tucker: *Reader,* p. 113.

65. ME, *Person,* p. 82.

66. DE, *Music,* p. 77.

67. As above, p. 124.

68. Stewart, *Boy,* p. 177.

69. Barry Ulanov, *Duke Ellington,* London 1947, p. 249.

70. DE, *Music,* p. 17. Robb Holmes's website is at www.ilinks.net/~holmesr/ duke.htm

71. DE, *Music,* p. 124.

72. Jazz at Ronnie Scott's magazine, issue 117, March-April 1999.

73. Constant Lambert, *Music Ho!* London 1934 (Penguin editon 1948 p162).

74. *Daily Herald,* 13 June, 1933.

75. Quoted in John Bird, *Percy Grainger,* London, 1982, p. 204.

76. *Daily Express,* 10 June 1933.

77. *Down Beat,* 5 November 1952, collected in Tucker, *Reader,* p. 268.

78. *Daily Express,* 12 January 1963.

79. Wilder Hobson, *'Fortune'* article, collected in Ralph de Toledano, *Frontiers of Jazz,* New York, 1947, p. 139.

80. Stewart, *Boy ,* p. 133.

81. as above, p. 149.

82. as above, p. 147.

83. Sigmund Spaeth, *A History of Popular Music in America,* London 1961, p. 498.

84. Interview with author, 2 February, 2005.

85. Interview with Patricia Willard, 16 November 1978. Smithsonian Institution Jazz Oral History Project, Institute of Jazz Studies, Rutgers.

86. *Down Beat,* February 1939, collected in Tucker, *Reader,* p. 133.

87. Richard O Boyer, *The Hot Bach,* *New Yorker,* 1944, collected in Tucker, *Reader,* p. 244.

88. *Down Beat,* November 1935, colected in Tucker, *Reader,* p 120.

89. Schuller, *The Swing Era,* New York, 1989, p. 83.

90. Interview in *Reminiscing in Tempo,* TV documentary by Robert S Levi, 1991.

91. ME, *Person,* p. 76.

92. Don George, *The Real Duke Ellington,* London 1981, p. 141.

93. Don George, *The Real Duke Ellington,* London 1981, p. 80.

94. Gunther Schuller, *The Swing Era,* New York, 1989, p. 133.

95. DE, *Music,* p. 156.

96. David Hajdu, *Lush Life,* London 1996 p. 66.

97. as above, p. 79.

98. Don George, *The Real Duke Ellington,* London 1981, , p. 79.

99. *Down Beat,* 5 November, 1952: collected in Tucker, *Reader,* p 270.

100. J Von Chapman, *Town Chatter, St Louis Argus,* 27 October 1939, quoted in Kenneth R Steiner, *On the Road and On the Air with Duke Ellingont,* 2004, pp. 1-2.

101. *In the Groove, Indianapolis Recorder,* 9 December 1939, in Steiner as above, pp. 2-3.

102. DE, *Music,* p. 164.

103. as above.

104. as above, p. 163.

105. Stanley Dance, *The World of Duke Ellingot,* London 1971, p. 35.

106. Richard O Boyer, *The Hot Bach,* in *The New Yorker,* 1944, collected in Tucker, *Reader,* p 235.

107. Stewart, *Boy,* p. 193.

108. Interview in BBC-TV documentary *Ridin on a Blue Note.*

109. Nicholson, *Portrait,* pp. 236-7.

110. Payroll sheets in Subsection 3A, Business Records, DEC.

111. Stewart, *Boy,* p. 193.

112. As above, p. 192.
113. Interview by Stan Britt, *First lady of Jazz,* Jazz Journal, 1 September 1981, quoted in Linda Dahl, *Morning Glory,* p 131.
114. DE, *Music,* p. 169.
115. Interview with author at the Institute of Jazz Studies, Rutgers University, 16 March 2005.
116. Richard O Boyer, *The Hot Bach,* in *The New Yorker,* 1944, collected in Tucker, *Reader,* p 218.
117. Nicholson, *Portrait,* p. 372.
118. Stewart, *Boy,* p. 164.
119. Richard O Boyer, *The Hot Bach,* in *The New Yorker,* 1944, collected in Tucker, *Reader,* p. 238.
120. ME, *Person,* p. 154.
121. Don George, *The Real Duke Ellingoton,* London 1981, p. 149.
122. Richard O Boyer, *The Hot Bach,* in *The New Yorker,* 1944, collected in Tucker, *Reader,* p. 215.
123. as above, p. 224.
124. Jewell, *Duke* , p. 101.
125. Bill Crow, *Jazz Anecdotes*, New York, 1990, p. 251.
126. Rex Stewart, *Jazz Masters of the Thirties,* p. 113.
127. Nicolson , *Portrait,* p. 230.
128. Don George, *The Real Duke Ellington,* London 1981, p. 20.
129. as above, p. 138.
130. Interview with Dr Marcia Greenlee in Washington DC, 26 March 1991, for Duke Ellington Oral History Project, Archives Center, National Museum of American History, Washington DC.
131. Interview with Milt Hinton, March 1980: Smithsonian Institution Jazz Oral History Project, Institute of Jazz Studies.
132. Don DeMichael: *Charlie Rouse: Artistry and Originalty*, Down Beat 25 May 1961, p. 18.
133. Jim Godbolt, *A History of Jazz in Britain, 1919–1950*, London, 1984, p. 118.

134. London *Evening Standard,* 11 March, 1939.
135. Leonard Feather, liner notes for Prestige P24102/3.
136. ME, *Person,* p. 102.
137. Quoted in Nicholson, *Portrait,* p 276.
138. Stewart, *Boy,* p. 193.
139. Peter Lavezzoli, *The King of All, Sir Duke.* New York & London 2001, pp. 43-44.
140. DE, *Music,* p. 226.
141. Peter J Levinson, *Trumpet Blues, The Life of Harry James,* New York, 1999, p. 179.
142. Eddie Lambert, *Duke Ellington, A Listener's Guide,* Lanham, Maryland, and London 1999, p 163.
143. DE, *Music,* p. 229.
144. as above, p. 189.
145. David Hajdu, *Lush Life,* London 1996 p. 141.
146. Alec Wilder, *American Popular Song,* New York, 1972, p. 415.
147. Stanley Dance, liner notes from Mosaic MD5-160.
148. David Hajdu, *Lush Life,* London 1996 p. 187.
149. Nicholson, *Portrait,* p. 301.
150. Derek Jewell: *Duke: A Portrait of Duke Ellington,* New York, 1977, p. 110.
151. George Wein with Nate Chinen, *Myself and Others,* Cambridge, MA., 2003, p. 151.
152. As above, p. 154.
153. DE, *Music,* p. 227.
154. George Wein with Nate Chinen, *Myself and Others,* Cambridge, MA., 2003 , p. 156.
155. DE, *Music,* p. 221.
156. Stanley Dance, *The World of Duke Ellingot,* London 1971, p 188.
157. DE, *Music,* p. 227 .
158. DE, *MM,* p. 226.
159. Eddie Lambert, *Duke Ellington, A Listener's Guide,* Lanham,

Maryland, and London 1999, p 191.

160. *Jazz Monthly,* January, 1964, collected in Max Harrison, *A Jazz Retrospect,* 2nd edn., London 1991, p. 124.

161. *Time,* 20 August 1956.

162. ME, *Person*, p. 109.

163. *Down Beat,* 7 March 1956.

164. David Hajdu, *Lush Life,* London, 1997, p. 147.

165. *Arts*, 1958. Collected in André Hodeir trans. Noel Burch, *Towards Jazz,* London 1965, p. 27.

166. David Hajdu, *Lush Life,* London, 1997, p. 154.

167. Nicholson, *Portrait*, p. 312-3.

168. Jewell: *Duke*, p. 123.

169. David Hajdu, *Lush Life,* London, 1997, p. 158.

170. as above, p. 155.

171. Walter van de Leur, *Someting to Live For,* New York, 2002, p. 134-5.

172. Nicholson, *Portrait,* p. 315.

173. DE, *Music*, p. 256.

174. Eddie Lambert, *Duke Ellington, A Listener's Guide,* Lanham, Maryland, and London 1999, p. 200.

175. *Daily Mail*, 6 October 1958.

176. *Daily Mail,* 3 March, 1961.

177. Derek Jewell, *Duke,* p. 133.

178. David Hajdu, *Lush Life,* p. 207.

179. J C Thomas, *Chasin' the Trane,* London 1976, p. 114.

180. Gene Santoro, *Myself When I am Real: The life and music of Charles Mingus,* New York, 2000, p. 199.

181. DE, *Muisc,* p. 196.

182. *Chicago Defender,* 27 July, 1960.

183. ME, *Person,* p. 126.

184. Don George, *The Real Duke Ellington,* London 1981, p. 142.

185. Jewell, *Duke*, p. 136.

186. ME, *Person*, p. 126-7.

187. Interview with author, 14 May, 2005.

188. Interview with author, 27 April, 2005.

189. ME, *Person,* , p. 128.

190. Nicholson,*Portrait,* p. 368.

191. DE, *Music,* p. 190.

192. Will Friedwald: *Sinatra! The Song is You,* New York, 1997, p. 306.

193. Marshall and Jean Stearns, *Jazz Dance,* New York, 1968, p. 352.

194. *Daily Mail,* 17 February, 1964.

195. Nicholson, *Portrait,* p. 353.

196. As above p. 354.

197. George Wein with Nate Chinen, *Myself Among Others,* Cambridge, Mass., 2003, p. 163.

198. Stanley Dance, liner notes to RCA PL45699, 1967.

199. Nat Hentoff, *This Cat Needs No Pulitzer Prize, New York Times magazine,* 12 September 1966, collected in Tucker, *DE Reader,* p. 362.

200. Jewell, *Duke*, p. 222.

201. David Hajdu, *Lush Life,* London 1997, p. 253.

202. as above, p. 254.

203. DE, *Music,* p. 159-161.

204. Jewell,Derek Jewell, *Duke*, New York 1977, p. 196.

205. Ralph Ellison, in *Sunday Star,* (Washington, DC) 27 April, 1969, reprinted in *Going to the Territory,* New York, 1986, pp. 217-26.

206. Quoted in Stanley Dance, liner note for RCA LSP 3906.

207. DE, *Music,* p. 288.

208. as above, pp. 267-8.

209. as above, p. 269.

210. ME, *Person*, p. 180.

211. Jewell, *Duke,* p. 177.

212. ME, *Person*, p. 203.

213. Quoted in Gore Vidal, *Armageddon?: Essays 1983-87,* London 1987, p. 5.

214. Jewell, *Duke,* p. 191.

215. as above.

216. Stewart, *Boy,* p. 209.

217. DE. *Music*, p. 119.

218. Eddie Lambert, *Duke Ellington, A Listener's Guide,* Lanham, Maryland, and London 1999, p. 313.

219. Letter dated 1 July 1971, from Joel C Bender, Attorney for National Recording Studios, in Subseries 3H, Business Records, DEC.

220. ME, p. 171.

221. Letter in Series 5, Personal Correspondence and Notes, DEC.

222. Nicolson, *Portrait,* p. 407.

223. Quoted in Jewell, *Duke,* p. 218.

224. Quoted in ME, *Person,* p. 196.

225. Jewell, *Duke,* p. 222.

226. as above, p. 223.

227. ME, *Person,* 198.

228. Jewell, *Duke* p. 224.

229. as above.

230. Jim Lowe interview with Dr Marca Greenlee, Washington DC, 9 March 1990, Smithsonian Institution Duke Ellington Oral History Project, Archives Center, National Museum of American History, Washington DC.

231. *A Visit with Mrs Ellington, Ebony,* March 1959, pp. 132-8.

Chronology

Year	Age	Life
1899		Born on 29 April in Washington, DC, to James Edward Ellington and Daisy Ellington, née Kennedy. He is named Edward Kennedy Ellington.
1906	7	First piano lessons with local teacher, Mrs Clinkscales: Edward prefers baseball.
1913	14	Enters Armstrong High School, studying graphic arts.
1914	15	On holiday in New Jersey, he hears the pianist Harvey Brooks, and becomes interested in piano. Meets Washington musicians at Frank Holliday's poolroom. Composes first piece,'Soda Fountain Rag'.
1915	16	Gets the nickname 'Duke'. His sister, Ruth, is born in August.
1916	17	Begins to work in bands in and around Washington.

Year	History	Culture
1899	In South Africa, Boer War. In France, Dreyfus is pardoned. Germany secures Baghdad Railroad contract.	Berlioz, *The Taking of Troy*. A. Dvorak, *Kate and the Devil*. E. Elgar, *Enigma Variations*.
1906	Duma created in Russia. Revolution in Iran.	Henri Matisse, *Bonheur de vivre*. Maxim Gorky, *The Mother* (until 1907).
1913	In US, Woodrow Wilson becomes president (until 1921). Hans Geiger invents Geiger counter.	Stravinsky, *The Rite of Spring*. Guillaume Apollinaire, *Les peintres cubistes*. D H Lawrence, *Sons and Lovers*. Marcel Proust, *A la recherche du temps perdu* (until 1927).
1914	28 June: Archduke Franz Ferdinand assassinated in Sarajevo. First World War begins. Panama Canal opens. Egypt becomes British protectorate.	James Joyce, *Dubliners*. Ezra Pound, *Des Imagistes*. Gustav Holst, *The Planets*.
1915	Dardanelles/Gallipoli campaign (until 1916). Italy denounces its Triple Alliance with Germany and Austria-Hungary.	Twelve-reel *Birth of a Nation*, first modern motion picture, grosses $18m. Picasso, Harlequin.
1916	Battle of Verdun.	German painter Franz Marc falls in the War.

Year	Age	Life
1917	18	Works with two friends, trumpeter Artie Whetsel and saxophonist Otto 'Toby' Hardwick. They play with Baltimore banjoist and leader Elmer Snowden. Ellington drops out of school.
1918	19	Forms The Duke's Serenaders. Marries his girl friend, Edna Thompson, on 2 July.
1919	20	A son, Mercer Kennedy Ellington, is born on 11 March. Ellington books bands and paints signs for dances.
1920	21	A second child dies at birth. Ellington performs for New York stride piano master James P Johnson, playing Johnson's test piece, 'Carolina Shout'.
1921	22	Ellington makes first visit to New York, with Snowden, Whetsel, Hardwick and drummer Sonny Greer. He meets the pianist Willie 'The Lion' Smith.

Year	History	Culture
1917	In Russia, Tsar Nicholas II abdicates: Communists seize power under Vladimir Lenin. US enters First World War. Balfour Declaration on Palestine: Britain favours creation of Jewish state without prejudice to non-Jewish communities.	First recording of New Orleans jazz. Franz Kafka, *Metamorphosis*. T S Eliot, Prufrock and *Other Observations*. Giurgio de Chirico, *Le Grand Métaphysique*.
1918	In Russia, Tsar Nicholas II and family executed. 11 November: Armistice agreement ends First World War. 'Spanish flu' epidemic kills at least 20m people in Europe, US and India.	Oswald Spengler, *The Decline of the West*, Volume 1. Amédée Ozenfant and Le Corbusier, *Après le Cubisme*. Paul Klee, *Gartenplan*.
1919	In US, prohibition begins. Irish Civil War (until 1921).	United Artists formed with Charlie Chaplin, Mary Pickford, Douglas Fairbanks and D W Grifith as partners.
1920	IRA formed. First meeting of League of Nations.	June: Provides score for *George White's Scandals of 1920*.
1921	Paris conference of wartime Allies fixes Germany's reparation payments: Rhineland occupied. National Economic Policy in Soviet Union.	Sergey Prokofiev, *The Love of Three Oranges*. Luigi Pirandello, *Six Characters in Search of an Author*. Chaplin, *The Kid*.

Year	Age	Life
1923	24	Joins clarinettist Wilbur Sweatman's band in New York with Greer and Hardwick; when work and money run out they return to Washington. In June the friends, with Whetsel and Snowden, are offered another job in New York, but it does not materialize. Under Snowden's leadership, they find work at the Exclusive Club in Harlem, then at the Hollywood Club, a.k.a. Kentucky Club, in midtown. Ellington replaces Snowden as leader, and the band is renamed The Washingtonians.
1924	25	A series of fires intermittently closes the club: and the band tours New England during rebuildings. Ellington begins to write songs with lyricist Jo Trent: they sell their song 'Pretty Soft for You'. With the trumpeter Bubber Miley and trombonist Charlie Irvis in the band, Ellington makes his first records as leader.
1925	26	The review 'Chocolate Kiddies', including songs by Ellington and Trent, opens in Germany. Ellington studies with the composers Will Marion Cook and Will Vodery.
1926	27	Trombonist Joe 'Tricky Sam' Nanton and bassist Wellman Braud join expanded band. Publisher Irving Mills takes over as manager. Ellington and Miley write 'East St Louis Toodle-oo,' the band's signature tune. Records for Vocalion.

Year	History	Culture
1923	Ottoman empire ends; Palestine, Transjordan and Iraq to Britain; Syria to France.	Le Corbusier, *Vers une architecture*.
1924	Vladimir Lenin dies. Greece is proclaimed a republic. Rioting between Hindus and Muslims in Delhi. Calvin Coolidge wins US presidential elections.	Forster, *A Passage to India*. Kafka, *The Hunger Artist*. Thomas Mann, *The Magic Mountain*. André Breton, first surrealist manifesto.
1925	Pact of Locarno, multilateral treaty intended to guarantee peace in Europe. Chiang Kai-shek launches campaign to unify China. Discovery of ionosphere.	Erik Satie dies. F Scott Fitzgerald, *The Great Gatsby*. Kafka, *The Trial*. Sergey Eisenstein, *Battleship Potemkin*. Television invented.
1926	Germany joins League of Nations. Hirohito becomes emperor of Japan.	Hemingway, *The Sun Also Rises*. A A Milne, *Winnie-the-Pooh*. Fritz Lang, *Metropolis*.

Year	Age	Life
1927	28	Records for Brunswick, Columbia, OKeh and Victor under various names. Writes 'Black and Tan Fantasy' and 'Creole Love Call', recorded with Adelaide Hall's wordless vocal. On 4 December, with reed-players Barney Bigard and Harry Carney in the band, Ellington opens at the Cotton Club in Harlem, accompanying a new revue with 'jungle music'. Broadcasts from the club spread his music across North America.
1928	29	Johnny Hodges joins on alto saxophone. Ellington records 'The Mooche' and 'Black Beauty'. He leaves Edna after she slashes his face because of his affair with actress Fredi Washington.
1929	30	Whetsel and Ellington appear with Fredi Washington in short fiction film 'Black and Tan Fantasy', made in New York. Band appears in Florenz Ziegfeld's revue, 'Show Girl'. Miley is fired for drunkenness and replaced by Cootie Williams. Juan Tizol joins on valve-trombone. Ellington moves his parents, sister and son to New York.

Year	History	Culture
1927	Joseph Stalin comes to power; Leon Trotsky expelled from Soviet Communist Party. Charles Lindbergh flies across Atlantic.	Martin Heidegger, *Being and Time*. Virginia Woolf, *To the Lighthouse*. BBC public radio launched.
1928	Kellogg-Briand Pact for Peace. Transjordan becomes self-governing under the British mandate. Albania is proclaimed a kingdom. Alexander Fleming discovers penicillin.	Maurice Ravel, *Boléro*. Kurt Weill, *The Threepenny Opera*. Huxley, *Point Counter Point*. D H Lawrence, *Lady Chatterley's Lover*. W B Yeats, *The Tower*. Walt Disney, *Steamboat Willie*.
1929	Wall Street crash. Young Plan for Germany.	First Academy Awards are announced.

Year	Age	Life
1930	31	Band appears on Broadway backing the French singing star Maurice Chevalier. In the Cotton Club's summer break it travels to Hollywood and appears in a feature film, 'Check and Double Check.'. Compositions include 'Mood Indigo' and 'Rockin' in Rhythm'.
1931	32	'Creole Rhapsody' is the first piece of popular music to fill both sides of a 10-inch 78 rpm record. Ellington ends his residency at the Cotton Club and begins touring. In Chicago, the singer Ivie Anderson joins the band: in Los Angeles the trombonist Lawrence Brown joins.
1932	33	Ivie Anderson makes her first record: 'It Don't Mean a Thing (If it Ain't Got that Swing)'. Ellington demonstrates jazz to Percy Grainger's class at Columbia University, New York.
1933	34	First tour of Europe, playing the Palladium in London and meeting members of the royal family, then playing Salle Pleyel in Paris.

Year	History	Culture
1930	Mahatma Gandhi leads Salt March in India. Frank Whittle patents turbo-jet engine. Pluto discovered.	The Hays Office institutes the Production Code guidelines of moral standards in the movies.
1931	King Alfonso XIII flees; Spanish republic formed. New Zealand becomes independent. Japan occupies Manchuria. Building of Empire State Building completed in New York.	Antoine de St-Exupéry, *Vol de nuit/Night Flight*. Rakhmaninov's music is banned in Soviet Union as 'decadent'. Chaplin, *City Lights*. Fritz Lang, *M. Frankenstein* starring Boris Karloff.
1932	Kingdom of Saudi Arabia independent. Kingdom of Iraq independent. James Chadwick discovers neutron. First autobahn opened, between Cologne and Bonn.	Aldous Huxley, *Brave New World*. Jules Romains, *Les homes de bonne volonté*. Bertolt Brecht, *The Mother.* Thomas Beecham founds London Philharmonic Orchestra.
1933	Adolf Hitler appointed German chancellor. F D Roosevelt president in US; launches New Deal.	André Malraux, *La condition humaine*. Gertrude Stein, *The Autobiography of Alice B Toklas*.

Year	Age	Life
1934	35	Band appears in two Hollywood features, 'Murder at the Vanities' and 'Belle of the Nineties', starring Mae West. Daisy Ellington moves back to Washington after contracting cancer. Ellington begins relationship with dancer Mildred Dixon. Rex Stewart joins on cornet.
1935	36	'Symphony in Black', a movie with a score compiled mainly from earlier Ellington pieces, and featuring Billie Holiday briefly singing the blues. In May, Daisy dies, and Ellington is devastated by grief. In September he records 'Reminiscing in Tempo' over four 78 sides, to commemorate Daisy.
1936	37	Composes 'Caravan' with Tizol.
1937	38	Irving Mills launches his own record labels, Master and Variety, and Ellington records for them: they fail within the year and are sold to Columbia. Ellington's father has treatment for the results of alcoholism. Ellington meets Dr Arthur Logan, who becomes his doctor and closest friend. He leaves Mildred Dixon and moves in with Evie Ellis, a Cotton Club showgirl. In December J E Ellington dies.

Year	History	Culture
1934	In China, Mao Zedong starts on the Long March. Enrico Fermi sets off first controlled nuclear reaction.	Shostakovich, *The Lady Macbeth of Mtsensk*. Agatha Christie, *Murder on the Orient Express*. Henry Miller, *Tropic of Cancer*.
1935	Mustafa Kemal, President of Turkey, adopts name of Kemal Atatürk. Chiang Kai-shek named President of Chinese executive. German Luftwaffe formed.	Marx Brothers, *A Night at the Opera*. G. Gershwin, *Porgy and Bess*. G. Orwell, *A Clergyman's Daughter*.
1936	Germany occupies Rhineland. Edward VIII abdicates throne in Britain; George VI becomes king. Spanish Civil War (until 1939).	RCA experiments with television broadcasts from the Empire State Building.
1937	Japan invades China: Nanjing massacre. Arab-Jewish conflict in Palestine.	Jean-Paul Sartre, *La Nausée*. John Steinbeck, *Of Mice and Men*. Picasso, *Guernica*.

Year	Age	Life
1938	39	Three Ellington men – Cootie Williams, Johnny Hodges and Harry Carney – play in Benny Goodman's Carnegie Hall concert. Ellington does not attend. At Pittsburgh on tour, Ellington meets the pianist and composer Billy Strayhorn.
1939	40	On second European tour, the Ellington band is refused work permits for Britain. It tours on the Continent, and Ellington celebrates his 40th birthday in Stockholm, later composing 'Serenade to Sweden.' Strayhorn joins the Ellington organization and collaborates on 'Something to Live For.' Jimmie Blanton joins on bass and Ben Webster on tenor.
1940	41	New contract with Victor, the only African-American band on its 75-cent premium label. Records include 'Ko-ko', 'Concerto for Cootie' , 'In a Mellotone', 'Jack the Bear', 'Cottontail', 'Dusk', 'Warm Valley'. Cootie Williams leaves to join Benny Goodman. Ray Nance, trumpet and violin, replaces him.

Year	History	Culture
1938	Kristallnacht: in Germany, Jewish houses, synagogues and schools are burnt down, and shops looted. Austrian Anschluss with Germany.	Warner Brothers produce *Confessions of a Nazi Spy*, although Germany represents 30% of the profits.
1939	1 September: Germany invades Poland. Francisco Franco becomes dictator of Spain. Britain and France declare war on Germany.	Steinbeck, *The Grapes of Wrath*. John Ford, *Stagecoach* (starring John Wayne). David O Selznick, *Gone with the Wind* (starring Vivien Leigh and Clark Gable).
1940	Germany occupies France, Belgium, the Netherlands, Norway and Denmark. In Britain, Winston Churchill becomes PM. Leon Trotsky assassinated in Mexico.	Graham Greene, *The Power and the Glory*. Ernest Hemingway, *For Whom the Bell Tolls*. Chaplin, *The Great Dictator*. Disney, *Fantasia*.

Year	Age	Life
1941	42	Dispute between song-writers' organisation ASCAP and radio stations over copyright payments leads to a ban on broadcasts of compositions by members, including Ellington. Strayhorn's piece, 'Take the "A" Train', becomes the band's signature tune, and Mercer, now a trained musician who has been leading his own band, contributes 'Things Ain't What They Used to Be' and other pieces to expand the band's repertoire for radio. In Los Angeles, 'Jump for Joy', a revue with music by Ellington, opens but does not do well enough to transfer to Broadway.
1942	43	On West Coast tour, Barney Bigard and singer Herb Jeffries leave, followed by Ivie Anderson. Jimmie Blanton dies of tuberculosis. American Federation of Musicians bans members from recording.
1943	44	At Carnegie Hall concert in January, Ellington premieres his multi-movement work about African-American history, 'Black, Brown and Beige'. Rex Stewart and Ben Webster leave and are replaced by Taft Jordan and Al Sears.
1944	45	Trumpeter Cart Anderson joins. Tizol leaves. In December, after Victor settles with AFM, Ellington records 'I'm Beginning to See the Light' and extracts from 'Black, Brown and Beige.'

Year	History	Culture
1941	Operation Barbarossa: Germany invades Soviet Union. In US, Lend-Lease Bill passed. Churchill and F D Roosevelt sign Atlantic Charter. Japan attacks Pearl Harbour: US enter Second World War. In US, Manhattan Project begins.	First commercial television station begins broadcasting. Fitzgerald's Hollywood novel, *The Last Tycoon*, is published posthumously.
1942	Japan invades Burma; captures Singapore. German General Rommel takes Tobruk; battle of El Alamein.	A. Camus, *L'Etranger*. Disney, *Bambi*. Popular Songs: 'The White Cliffs of Dover', 'White Christmas'.
1943	Allies bomb Germany. Allies invade Italy: Mussolini deposed. Albert Hoffman discovers hallucinogenic properties of LSD.	Rodgers and Hammerstein, *Oklahoma*. Sartre, *Being and Nothingness*. T S Eliot, *Four Quartets*.
1944	Allies land in Normandy: Paris is liberated. Civil war in Greece.	*Lay My Burden Down* (documentary about former slaves). Adorno and Horkheimer's essay on the 'Culture Industry'

Year	Age	Life
1945	46	Ellington begins broadcasts selling Victory Bonds on behalf of U.S. Treasury Department. Russell Procope joins the band.
1946	47	Otto Hardwick leaves. 'Tricky Sam' Nanton dies. Ellington signs with Musicraft Records, but the label has to buy back his contract and folds. In December 'Beggar's Holiday' a new version of 'The Beggar's Opera' with music by Ellington and Strayhorn, opens on Broadway but fails to draw a satisfactory audience.
1947	48	Liberia commissions 'The Liberian Suite' for the anniversary of its foundation, and Ellington plays it at Carnegie Hall. Rejoins Columbia records.
1948	49	Ellington takes Ray Nance and singer Kay Davis to Europe, avoiding ban on American musicians in Britain by appearing as a variety act with a London-based rhythm section.
1949	50	Guitarist Fred Guy leaves after 25 years.

Year	History	Culture
1945	8 May: 'V E Day'. General election in Britain brings Labour landslide. 14 August: Japan surrenders, end of World War II.	B. Britten, *Peter Grimes*. G. Orwell, *Animal Farm*. K. Popper, *The Open Society and Its Enemies*.
1946	In Argentina, Juan Perón becomes president. In India, Bombay legally removes discrimination against "untouchables". In Britain, National Health Service founded. Winston Churchill makes 'Iron Curtain' speech.	Bertrand Russell, *History of Western Philosophy*. Sartre, *Existentialism and Humanism*. Eugene O'Neill, *The Iceman Cometh*. Jean Cocteau, *La Belle et la Bête*.
1947	Truman Doctrine: US promises economic and military aid to countries threatened by Soviet expansion plans. India becomes independent. Chuck Yeager breaks the sounds barrier.	Tennessee Williams, *A Streetcar named Desire*. Albert Camus, *The Plague*. Anne Frank, *The Diary of Anne Frank*.
1948	Marshall plan (until 1951). Soviet blockade of Western sectors of Berlin: US and Britain organize airlift. In South Africa, Apartheid legislation passed. Gandhi is assassinated. State of Israel founded.	Brecht, *The Caucasian Chalk Circle*. Greene, *The Heart of the Matter*. Norman Mailer, *The Naked and the Dead*. Alan Paton, *Cry, the Beloved Country*. Vittorio De Sica, *Bicycle Thieves*.
1949	NATO formed. Republic of Ireland formed. Mao proclaims China a People's Republic.	George Orwell, *1984*. Simone de Beauvoir, *The Second Sex*. Arthur Miller, *Death of a Salesman*.

Year	Age	Life
1950	51	Tour of Europe, excluding Britain. Paul Gonsalves joins on tenor saxophone.
1951	52	Johnny Hodges leaves to lead his own band, taking Lawrence Brown and Sonny Greer. In 'The Great James Robbery', Ellington hires lead alto Willie Smith, trombonist Juan Tizol and drummer Louie Bellson from Harry James band. Premiere of 'Harlem'.
1953	54	Louie Bellson leaves to work with his wife, singer Pearl Bailey. Ellington joins Capitol Records and records 'Satin Doll,' his last big hit, but without lyrics: they are added in 1958.
1955	56	Season with Eliot Murphy's 'Aquashow' at the Flushing Meadow amphitheatre in New York suburbs, to keep band together. Hodges rejoins: Sam Woodyard comes in on drums. Capitol deal ends.
1956	57	Triumphant comeback starts with Gonsalves's marathon performance of 'Diminuendo and Crescendo in Blue' at Newport Jazz Festival, Rhode Island. Ellington on cover of 'Time' magazine. Agrees with Strayhorn that they will share credits from now on. New deal with Columbia.

Year	History	Culture
1950	Schuman Plan. Korean War begins. China conquers Tibet. Stereophonic sound invented. First successful kidney transplant.	In US, McCarthyism starts (to 1954). Billy Wilder, *Sunset Boulevard*.
1951	Anzus pact in Pacific.	J D Salinger, *The Catcher in the Rye*.
1953	Stalin dies. Mau Mau rebellion in Kenya. Eisenhower becomes US president. Korean War ends. Francis Crick and James Watson discover double helix (DNA).	Dylan Thomas, *Under Milk Wood*. Arthur Miller, *The Crucible*. Federico Fellini, *I Vitelloni*.
1955	West Germany joins NATO. Warsaw Pact formed.	Tennessee Williams, *Cat on a Hot Tin Roof*. Vladimir Nabokov, *Lolita*.
1956	Nikita Khruschev denounces Stalin. Suez Crisis. Revolts in Poland and Hungary. Fidel Castro and Ernesto 'Che' Guevara land in Cuba. Transatlantic telephone service links US to UK.	Lerner (lyrics) and Loewe (music), *My Fair Lady*. Elvis Presley, 'Heartbreak Hotel', 'Hound Dog', 'Love Me Tender'. John Osborne, *Look Back in Anger*.

Year	Age	Life
1957	58	Television musical 'A Drum is a Woman'. Suite based on Shakespearian characters for festival at Stratford, Ontario: 'Such Sweet Thunder.'
1958	59	Tours Britain in exchange for U.S. tour of trombonist Ted Heath's band: presented to Queen Elizabeth II at Leeds Festival.
1959	60	Records 'The Queen's Suite' and has only two copies pressed: one for the Queen, one for himself. Scores and appears in Otto Preminger courtroom drama, 'Anatomy of a Murder'.
1960	61	During a residency in Las Vegas, Ellington meets entertainer Fernanda de Castro Monte: she becomes his mistress, though he does not leave Evie. Lawrence Brown returns to the band. 'Suite Thursday', inspired by John Steinbeck novel 'Sweet Thursday' about the Monterey area, is premiered at Monterey Jazz Festival in September. Composes score for feature movie 'Paris Blues', starring Paul Newman, Sydney Poitier and featuring Louis Armstrong.

Year	History	Culture
1957	Treaty of Rome: EEC formed. USSR launches Sputnik 1. Ghana becomes independent.	The Academy excludes anyone on the Hollywood blacklist from consideration for Oscars (to 1959).
1958	Fifth French Republic; Charles De Gaulle becomes president. Great Leap Forward launched in China (until 1960). Castro leads communist revolution in Cuba.	Boris Pasternak, *Dr Zhivago*. Claude Lévi-Strauss, *Structural Anthropology*. Harold Pinter, *The Birthday Party*.
1959	In US, Alaska and Hawaii are admitted to the union. Solomon Bandaranaike, PM of Ceylon (Sri Lanka), is assassinated.	In Detroit, Berry Gordy founds Motown Records. Buddy Holly dies in plane crash. *Ben Hur* (dir. William Wyler). Günter Grass, *The Tin Drum*.
1960	Vietnam War begins (until 1975). OPEC formed. Oral contraceptives marketed.	Fellini, *La Dolce Vita*. Alfred Hitchcock, *Psycho*.

Year	Age	Life
1961	62	Records small-group sessions with Armstrong and Coleman Hawkins, and a 'battle of the bands' with Count Basie. Four band members arrested in drugs raid in Las Vegas.
1962	63	Cootie Williams rejoins. Ellington records trio album with two modernist musicians, bassist Charles Mingus and drummer Max Roach.
1963	64	Writes 'My People', a pageant for the Century of Negro Progress exposition in Chicago. Meets Martin Luther King Jr. Tours Middle East and Indian sub-continent for US State Department. Signs with Frank Sinatra's new label, Reprise. Records Swedish singer Alice Babs in Paris.
1964	65	Tour of Japan. Mercer Ellington joins band as road manager and fourth trumpet.
1965	66	'First Sacred Concert' at Grace Cathedral, San Francisco. Pulitzer Prize music jury proposes a special award for Ellington, but the governing committee rejects it.
1966	67	Tours in Europe, Africa and Japan. Records 'Far East Suite'. Performs 'First Sacred Concert' at Coventry Cathedral, one of many performance. Edna Ellington dies of cancer.

Year	History	Culture
1961	Berlin Wall erected. Bay of Pigs invasion. Yuri Gagarin is first man in space.	The Rolling Stones are formed. Rudolf Nureyev defects from USSR.
1962	Cuban missile crisis. Jamaica, Trinidad and Tobago, and Uganda become independent. Satellite television launched.	Edward Albee, *Who's Afraid of Virginia Woolf?* David Lean, *Lawrence of Arabia.*
1963	J F Kennedy assassinated; Martin Luther King leads March on Washington. Kenya becomes independent. Organisation of African Unity formed.	Betty Friedan, *The Feminine Mystique.* The Beatles, 'She Loves You'. *Cleopatra* (Richard Burton and Elizabeth Taylor). Luchino Visconti, *The Leopard.*
1964	Khruschev ousted by Leonid Brezhnev. First race relations act in Britain. Civil Rights Act in US. PLO formed. Word processor invented.	Harnick (lyrics) and Bock (music) *Fiddler on the Roof.* Saul Bellow, *Herzog.* Stanley Kubrick, *Doctor Strangelove.*
1965	Military coup in Indonesia.	Neil Simon, *The Odd Couple.*
1966	France withdraws its troops from NATO. In the US, race riots. Smith declares Rhodesia a republic.	John Lennon speculates that the The Beatles are more popular than Jesus. The group give their last concert.

Year	Age	Life
1967	68	Billy Strayhorn dies. Ellington records a memorial album of Strayhorn music, 'And his Mother Called Him Bill.'
1968	69	'Second Sacred Concert' given its premiere at Cathedral of St John the Divine, New York, with Alice Babs. Ellington and Strayhorn win Grammy for 'Far East Suite'. Jimmy Hamilton leaves. Ellington tours Mexico and Latin America.
1969	70	On Ellington's 70th birthday, President Richard M Nixon gives him the Medal of Freedom at a dinner in the White House.
1970	71	Premier of 'New Orleans Suite' at New Orleans Jazz Festival. Johnny Hodges dies. Lawrence Brown leaves. Ellington composes 'The River' for Alvin Ailey and American Ballet Company.
1971	72	Tours include first visit to Soviet Union.

Year	History	Culture
1967	Six day War between Israel and the Arab states. First heart transplant.	The Beatles, *Sergeant Pepper's Lonely Hearts Club Band*. Gabriel García Márquez, *One Hundred Years of Solitude*. Tom Stoppard, *Rosencrantz and Guildenstern are Dead*.
1968	Tet Offensive. In US, M L King and Robert Kennedy assassinated. In Paris, student riots.	Kubrick, *2001: A Space Odyssey*. The Rolling Stones, *Beggar's Banquet*.
1969	Neil Armstrong takes first moon walk. Internet created by US Department of Defence. Massive anti-war rallies in US.	Mario Puzo, *The Godfather*. *Easy Rider* (Dennis Hopper and Peter Fonda). *Midnight Cowboy* becomes first wide-released X-rated film.
1970	First-ever meeting of East and West German heads of government. In Cambodia: Prince Sihanouk is overthrown, US troops withdraw and Khmer Rouge takes over.	Simon and Garfunkel, *Bridge Over Troubled Water*. The Beatles officially split up. Death from drug overdose of guitarist Jimi Hendrix.
1971	In Uganda, Idi Amin seizes power. Nixon proclaims end of US offensive role in Vietnam War.	Dmitri Shostakovich, *Symphony No. 15*. Solzhenitsyn, *August 1914*. Kubrick, *A Clockwork Orange*.

Year	Age	Life
1972	73	Tour of Japan, Philippines, Thailand, Singapore, Indonesia, Australasia.
1973	74	'Third Sacred Concert', again with Alice Babs, given at Westminster Abbey. Ellington plays Royal Command performance at the Palladium in London. Tours Zambia and Ethiopia: Haile Selassie gives him the Emperor's Star. His memoir, 'Music is My Mistress', is published. Dr Arthur Logan dies in a fall from a bridge.
1974	75	Ellington collapses from cancer and is flown back to New York from Detroit. He goes into hospital and works on his comic opera, 'Queenie Pie'. He celebrates his 75th birthday in his room at the Harkness Pavilion of Columbia Presbyterian Hospital, and at 3.10 a.m. on 24 May, he dies there.

Year	History	Culture
1972	In US, Watergate scandal. Bloody Sunday massacre (N Ireland). Allende overthrown in Chile; Pinochet takes power. World Trade Centre completed. Optical fibre is invented.	Richard Adams, *Watership Down*. Bertolucci, *Last Tango in Paris*. Francis Ford Coppola, *The Godfather*.
1973	Yom Kippur War. Denmark, Ireland and Britain enter EC. US withdraws from Vietnam War. OPEC oil crisis.	Pink Floyd, *The Dark Side of the Moon*. Larkin, *High Windows*. E F Schumacher, *Small is Beautiful*. Truffaut, *Day for Night*.
1974	Watergate scandal; US President Richard Nixon forced to resign. Cyprus invaded by Turkey. Haile Selassie deposed in Ethiopia.	Dario Fo, *Can't Pay? Won't Pay!* Solzhenitsyn is expelled from the Soviet Union.

Further Reading

The most approachable biography of Duke Ellington is 'Beyond Category: The Life and Genius of Duke Ellington' by John Edward Hasse (New York, 1993): it benefits from his intimate knowledge of the Ellington archive for which he has responsibility at the Smithsonian Institution's National Museum of American History in Washington, DC. Stuart Nicolson's 'Reminiscing in Tempo: A Portrait of Duke Ellington' (London, 1999) tells his story through interviews, chiefly in the collections of the Smithsonian and the Institute of Jazz Studies. Derek Jewell, who wrote about jazz for the London *Sunday Times*, based his 'Duke: A Portrait of Duke Ellington' (London and New York , 1977) on his own conversations with Ellington. 'Sweet Man: The Real Duke Ellington', by Don George (NY, 1981) is a reminiscence by one of Ellington's lyric-writers, who shared his fascination with women.

For Ellington's biography before the Cotton Club days, Mark Tucker's 'Ellington: The Early Years' (Urbana, 1991) is an unparalleled work of scholarship and diligence which should have been the first volume of a definitive biography. Sadly, Tucker died before he could continue his work. He did, however, edit 'The Duke Ellington Reader' (New York, 1993), which collects important criticism, rapportage and interviews. Klaus Stratemann's monumental 'Duke Ellington, Day by Day and Film by Film' (Copenhagen, 1992) traces his movements in his professional life after late 1929, with many illustrations. Ken Vail's 'Duke's Diary' in two volumes covering the years up to and after 1950 (Cambridge, 1999 and Lanham, Maryland, 2002) also follows

Ellington's career, with valuable reprints of news reports, reviews, advertisements and photographs.

Duke Ellington's own memoir, 'Music is my Mistress', (NY 1974) is fascinating but not reliable, a collection of anecdotes and pen portraits rather than an autobiography. It was assembled from Ellington's often chaotic notes by Stanley Dance, who frequently acted as his press agent. Mercer Ellington had the collaboration of Dance on his book, 'Duke Ellington in Person: An intimate Memoir' (Boston and London 1978), and Dance wrote 'The World of Duke Ellington' (New York, 1970) a collection of interviews with Ellington's associates.

A ground-breaking biography of Billy Strayhorn is David Hajdu's 'Lush Life' (New York 1996): Walter van de Leur analysed Strayhorn's contribution to the Ellington band repertoire and his musical activities away from the Ellington circle in 'Something to Life For' (New York, 2002). Rex Stewart's autobiography, edited by Claire P Gordon, is 'Boy Meets Horn (Ann Arbor, 1991), and his magazine articles were collected as 'Jazz Masters of the Thirties' (New York and London, 1972). Willie 'The Lion' Smith's reminiscences are in 'Music on My Mind: The Memoirs of an American Pianist' (Garden City, NY, 1964)

'Duke Ellington: A Listener's Guide' (Lanham, Maryland, 1999) is a labour of love by the British Ellington expert Eddie Lambert, a record-by-record study of Ellington's output which is invaluable to anyone approaching the bewildering quantity of the Ellington discography.

André Hodeir's pioneering analysis of 'Concerto for Cootie' is in his 'Jazz: Evolution and Essence' (English translation, revised edn. New York, 1980). Gunther Schuller deals with the more technical aspects of Ellington's achievements in his ' Early Jazz' (New York, 1968) and 'The Swing Era' (New York, 1989). Dan Morgenstern's illuminating essays on various aspects of Ellington's work are in his collection 'Living With Jazz' (New York, 2004).

Gary Giddins's 'Visions of Jazz' (New York, 1998) includes his thoughts on the Sacred Concerts, on which he is far more positive than most critics; an early version of the chapter is in Tucker's 'Reader'. Although some of the above are out of print, others have been re-issued by Da Capo Press (www.dacapo.com).

There is a helpful bibliography maintained by Jazz Instutut at Darmstadt, Germany, on its website at jazzinsititutedarmstadt.de. The various Duke Ellington societies dedicated to performance, promotion and research into Ellington's music and career can be reached through the internet. The Duke Ellington Society (UK) is at www.dukes-place.co.uk. The International Duke Ellington Music Society Bulletin, edited by Sjef Hoefsmit, assisted by Roger Boyes, is at www.depanorama.net/dems. The Duke Ellington Society, based in New York, is at http://thedukeellingtonsociety.org. A compilation of many sites related to Ellington is at www.ellingtonweb.ca/

Listening

Duke Ellington's legacy of recordings was vast, and ownership of the original recordings has changed over the years. The unpredictable behaviour of record companies makes it difficult to be precise about what is available, so this is a general guide. Beginners wanting a selection of Ellington records will see that the bargain Naxos label has issued eight CDs of selected tracks made for various labels between the years 1927 and 1942, in respectable sound. JSP has launched what appears to be a more inclusive series: Volume 1, 'Mrs Clinkscales to the Cotton Club' uses four CDs to cover the period from 1926 to 1929, also at bargain prices. 'Early Ellington: The Original Decca recordings' (Decca/GRP) collects Brunswick and Vocalion issues between 1926 and 1931 in superior transfers on three CDs, including alternate takes. Less complete collections of the contemporary Victor and OKeh sides – Ellington sometimes recorded the same piece for several labels, using pseudonyms – are on Bluebird/BMG and Columbia/Legacy.

The 30s band is on 'Duke', a box set from Columbia, and 'The Duke: The Columbia Years 1927–1962' surveys the whole of his career with that label over three CDs. Two pairs of double-CD boxes on Columbia bring together most of the small-group sessions before the move to Victor.

Bluebird have remastered the most important part of Ellington's legacy on a three-CD box, 'Never No Lament: The Blanton – Webster Band', carrying 75 tracks, recorded from 1940 to 1942. Beware of earlier Bluebird attempts to put out the same material on CD: the sound was dull because of mistaken attempts to remove the surface noise of the original 78s. The same label's 'Centennial Collection' has a CD, superbly remastered by Steven Lasker, beginning with 'Black And Tan Fantasy' from October 1927 and including key pieces such as 'Ko-ko' and 'Dusk', plus seven previously unreleased recordings from 1941 broadcasts. The accompanying DVD has the film 'Symphony in Black' and seven videos of the band, plus an 11-minute 1941 audio interview with Ellington. The French Dreyfus label has two CDs, 'Ko-ko' and 'Take the "A" Train', with excellent transfers of material from 1938 to 1950. Bluebird also issued small groups on 'The Great Ellington Units' and the duets with bassist Jimmy Blanton on 'Solos, Duets and Trios'.

The 1943 Carnegie Hall concert, with the only complete recording Ellington made of 'Black, Brown and Beige', is on Prestige, and later Carnegie concerts are on Prestige and Ember. The Fargo concert is on Storyville, and the same label is reissuing the Treasury series of broadcasts in a series of double CDs.

'The Collection: '46-47 Recordings', on three Hindsight CDs, brings together transcriptions made for radio stations rather than for retail sale. Some of the earlier World Broadcasting Service transcriptions are available on Circle.

The Capitol album 'Ellington '55' plus a couple of extra tracks in on Blue Note: so are the sessions with Louis Armstrong and 'Money Jungle' the trio with Charles Mingus and Max Roach. The Reprise records under Ellington's name are in a box from Rhino/Warners.

The later Columbia recordings are being re-issued on Columbia/Legacy: they include 'Such Sweet Thunder', 'Ellington Uptown', 'Ellington at Newport', 'Piano in the Background', Piano in the Foreground'; and the exciting 'Blues in Orbit', which brings Jimmy Hamilton to the fore as a tenor soloist. The 'Far East Suite' and the Strayhorn memorial album 'And His Mother Called Him Bill' are on BMG/Bluebird. The 'New Orleans Suite' is on Atlantic. The 'Second Sacred Concert', or at least most if it, is on Prestige.

Original Jazz Classics put out 'Latin American Suite', 'Afro-Eurasian Eclipse' and, on a CD called 'The Ellington Suites', a collection of 'The Queen's Suite', 'The Goutelas Suite' from 1971, and 'The UWIS Suite' from 1972. Some of these recordings originated in the 'stockpile': the Danish label, Storyville, is issuing more material from it which Mercer Ellington handed over to Danish radio, most recently 'The Jaywalker' from 1966-7, including incidental music for a play, and 'True Piano Player', emphasising solo recordings.

The Paris-based Classics label has been putting out all of Ellington's studio recordings, except for alternative takes, as they fall out of copyright: they range over all the labels in chronological order, though after more than 15 years of production Classics still thinks it is spelt 'chronogical'. The sound quality is variable.

Acknowledgements

Many thanks for invaluable help goes to the following people and the institutions with which they are connected: Dr John Edward Hasse, Curator of American Music, and the staff of the Archives Center which includes the Duke Ellington Collection at the National Museum of American History, Smithsonian Institution, Washington DC; Dan Morgenstern, Director, and the staff of the Institute of Jazz Studies, Rutgers University, Newark, NJ, especially Annie Kuebler, Archivist; David Nathan of the National Jazz Archive, Loughton, Essex; Dr Wolfram Knauer, Director, and the staff of the Jazz-Institut Darmstadt, Germany; the staff of the National Sound Archive, British Library; Vic Bellerby, chairman, George Duncan, general secretary, and my fellow-members of the Duke Ellington Society (UK); Göran Wallén, chairman of the Duke Ellington Society Sweden, and the other organisers of the International Duke Ellington Conference in Stockholm, 2004.

My thanks also to the following individuals who provided information or advice: George Avakian, Mark Cantor, John Chilton, Kevin Henriques, Jeremy Hornsby, Michael Kilpatrick, Steven Lasker, Stuart O'Connor, Ted O'Reilly, Michael Peacock, Brian Peerless, Mike and Viv Phillips, Brian Priestly, Dermot Purgavie, Chuck Reed, Tom Rosenthal, Andrew Sheppard, Chris Sheridan, Kenneth R Steiner, Ken Vail, Larry Westland.

Once again old friends who have my particular gratitude include two clarinettists: Wally Fawkes for another beautiful cover and Kenny Davern for his stimulating encouragement. I am deeply grateful to Roger Boyes for agreeing to read the text, and to Peter Symes for his picture research.

My wife, Jane Mays, has been kind, generous, and sympathetic and to her, as ever, go my thanks and love.

Naturally, nobody but me is to blame for any errors.

Picture Sources

The author and publishers wish to express their thanks to the following sources of illustrative material and/or permission to reproduce it. They will make proper acknowledgements in future editions in the event that any omissions have occurred.

Chuck Stewart: pp. 61, 83, 106; Frank Driggs Collection: pp. 9, 13, 18 (Photo by Duncan Butler), 22, 23, 29, 35 (Photo by Henry Delorval Green), 38, 41, 43 (Photo by Duncan Butler), 45, 50 (Photo by Duncan Butler), 69, 70, 75, 86, 89 (Photo by Duncan Butler), 111; Getty Images: pp. vi, 5, 92, 101, 119, 125, 130; Kendall/Bolden Collection/Symil Library: p 25; Mike Doyle / Symil Library: p. 116; Charles Peterson, courtesy of Don Peterson: p. 59.

Index